BEST RUNS

JOE HENDERSON

West Coast Editor, *Runner's World* Magazine
Editor, *Running Commentary* Newsletter

Human Kinetics

Library of Congress Cataloging-in-Publication Data

Henderson, Joe, 1943-
    Best runs / Joe Henderson.
      p. cm.
    Includes index.
    ISBN 0-88011-896-2 (paperback)
    1. Running--Training.   2. Running races. I. Title.
    GV1061.5.H45   1999
     796.42--dc21   98-7281
                                              CIP

ISBN: 0-88011-896-2
Copyright © 1999 by Joe Henderson

Acquisitions Editor: Martin Barnard; **Developmental Editor:** Julie Rhoda; **Assistant Editors:** Sandra Merz Bott and Cassandra Mitchell; **Copyeditor:** Stephen Moore; **Proofreader:** Myla Smith; **Indexer:** Craig Brown; **Graphic Designer:** Robert Reuther; **Graphic Artist:** Tara Welsch; **Photo Editor:** Boyd LaFoon; **Cover Designer:** Jack Davis; **Photographer (cover):** New England Stock/Gregg Adams; **Photographer (interior):** Photos on pages 20, 27, 108, 119, 136, 164, and 173 © Human Kinetics/Tom Roberts; **Printer:** Versa Press

Human Kinetics books are available at special discounts for bulk purchase. Special editions or book excerpts can also be created to specification. For details, contact the Special Sales Manager at Human Kinetics.

Printed in the United States of America   10 9 8 7 6 5 4 3 2 1

Human Kinetics
Web site: http://www.humankinetics.com/

United States: Human Kinetics, P.O. Box 5076, Champaign, IL 61825-5076
1-800-747-4457
e-mail: humank@hkusa.com

Canada: Human Kinetics, 475 Devonshire Road Unit 100, Windsor, ON N8Y 2L5
1-800-465-7301 (in Canada only)
e-mail: humank@hkcanada.com

Europe: Human Kinetics, P.O. Box IW14, Leeds LS16 6TR, United Kingdom
(44) 1132 781708
e-mail: humank@hkeurope.com

Australia: Human Kinetics, 57A Price Avenue, Lower Mitcham, South Australia 5062
(088) 277 1555
e-mail: humank@hkaustralia.com

New Zealand: Human Kinetics, P.O. Box 105-231, Auckland 1
(09) 523 3462
e-mail: humank@hknewz.com

To Browning Ross,
who led me into longer running and published
my first writing

Contents

PART I   Best Ways   1

1   Picking the Best Bets 3

Fifty Is Nifty • Time Trials • Weird Ideas That Work • Best Answers

2   Training by the Numbers 13

Start With Cooper • Twice as Nice • Balancing Act • Far, Fast, Fresh

3   Learning How to Walk 23

Walk Talk • Walk Wars • Stopping and Drinking • Walking Lessons

4   Running Out of Time 33

Shouting Softly • Honest Efforts • Timeless Racing • Time Out

5   Listening to the Heart 41

Checking Your Pulse • Your Own Best Beat • Extra Efforts • Three-Part Harmony

Foreword

Joe Henderson and I have been running together for a long time, well over half of our lives. We first lined up together at the 1967 Boston Marathon, though we didn't know each other yet.

The following year I won at Boston, and Joe started writing his column for *Distance Running News* (the precursor to *Runner's World*). He was also at work on his first book, *Long Slow Distance*, in which he gave me a chance to tell my personal story. Unfortunately, I was so busy logging more than 100 miles per week that I missed Joe's deadline. Somehow he coped with my tardiness and figured out a way to fit my contribution into his book. Through this experience, I learned something about Joe that I've witnessed many times since. He's a man of great calmness and patience who will nevertheless stretch any boundaries to fit the latest information into his books.

Joe edited *Runner's World* through the 1970s, and he assigned me my first article for the magazine. This experience convinced me to give up my job as a schoolteacher and to take the plunge into the running business full-time. In a sense, Joe was my first boss. He then gave up editing to spend more time with his first love, writing. And he writes voluminously—in a daily journal, in letters and e-mail messages by the dozens, in his magazine columns, newsletter, and in books such as this.

I now sit in the chair he once occupied as *Runner's World* editor, which you might say now makes me Joe's boss. But neither of us thinks of it that way. We are teammates and have been for a long time. I've been reading his writings for more than 30 years.

To my way of thinking, Joe's words and attitude have encouraged as many runners as the best-selling authors Jim Fixx (who featured Joe in his first book) and George Sheehan (whom Joe edited). I say "attitude" because Joe's books have two equally important parts. First, of course, he conveys the kind of information that runners need to know. Nobody knows more than Joe or writes about it more clearly. But information is just information. It's an easy-to-get commodity in this digital age. When I read Joe's work in the early 1970s, it was his attitude that impressed me most and inspired me to more and better running. For me, the best part of his writing is the way he expresses his love of running and his understanding that running is a totally individualistic activity.

Joe will tell you how to run and even provide some reasons to run, but mainly he'll tell you to run for whatever reason moves you. And he'll affirm that your reasons, whatever they might be, are just as important as anyone else's. You don't have to be chasing an Olympic gold medal. Find your own meaning, and you'll find your own rewards.

As consistent as Joe's writing has been over the decades, it has also evolved. He has gone from young editor of *Runner's World* to our senior columnist, from fairly serious racer to relaxed older runner. He has aged yet has kept up with running. This book reflects his latest thinking. It includes some of his best writing yet. As you turn the pages, I'm sure you'll find yourself nodding in agreement, thinking, "Yes, that's just the way I feel, too."

At his desk, Joe is a writer and editor. In these pages, you'll find him also to be a friend and training partner. And you'll be glad to have him along with you on runs.

Amby Burfoot
Editor, *Runner's World*

Acknowledgments

Books credit only their authors on the cover and spine, but this writing wasn't an individual sport. The bylined writer's work could never have reached print without assists from many teammates.

This book was first the idea of Martin Barnard at Human Kinetics. He asked me to put together an all-new sequel to *Better Runs*, which HK had published in 1995. Julie Rhoda, Sandra Merz Bott, and Tara Welsch later took charge of polishing my manuscript into the form you see it now.

Behind each of the book's pieces stand sources of material and inspiration, which usually are named in the text. Most of the writing here began life as columns in my newsletter *Running Commentary* and in *Runner's World* magazine. Barbara Shaw and Janet Heinonen clean up the newsletter pieces each month before they go into print. Amby Burfoot provides monthly space to me in the magazine, and Cristina Negron selects and corrects the material to fill it. Readers then tell me what they like or not in this material, thereby voting on what qualifies for book consideration.

There couldn't have been a *Best Runs* without my teammates. I thank and credit you all.

Introduction: Best Words

John Steinbeck, my first writing hero, said he wasn't ready to write a book until he could tell what it was about in one sentence. My requirement is even tighter. I can't start until my book's theme can fit into the few words of a title.

Just two words—Best Runs—draw this book's starting line, and the content hinges on the first of them. *Best* needs some defining and explaining so I'll know how to fill the book and you'll know what to expect from it. My dictionary's first definition of that word is "excelling all others." But I'm now more fond of the second: "most productive of good or of advantage, utility or satisfaction."

Most runners start out by measuring their efforts against that first definition. The best runs are those ending with the same final three letters as best: farthest in distance and fastest in time, of course, but also the hardest effort, the toughest courses, and the harshest weather.

Establishing and exceeding personal bests is important to runners still in their improvement cycle. They need these *-est* mileposts as motivators and as rewards. But this is a limiting way of defining best. We can't always and forever take superlative runs.

Each new PR (personal record) makes the next one harder to set, and improvement seldom extends more than 10 years. Then what keeps the runner motivated and rewarded? Fortunately, there's that second definition of best. It doesn't rely on "excelling all others" but on being the most satisfying in less dramatic ways.

In the late 1970s I wrote a book titled *Run Farther, Run Faster*. I was in my mid-30s then and, without yet knowing it, had just set my last personal-best time—a cheap one at a seldom-run event. My PR for longest distance ever covered in a race was also relatively new then. That book defined best in the way most runners did at the time. They judged it entirely by race results.

Now it's the late 1990s, and I'm in my mid-50s. If my youngest PR were my child, it would be old enough to take a legal drink. My running moves much slower than it did 20 years ago, and for lesser distances. But as these runs purr along quietly, they're in other ways the best they have ever been. What I lost in speed and length, I've gained many times over from learning that most runs can be "productive of good."

Best no longer means the ultimates that could only be found rarely. It has come to mean the favorites that I can visit anytime. If you're still looking for your ultimate runs, you might get some help here but will likely find more in other books. I fill this one with the second type of best runs, and with my favorite writings on this subject.

Best Runs resembles its Human Kinetics predecessor, *Better Runs*, in three ways: in format (combining more than 100 short essays), in source (all written originally as magazine and newsletter columns), and in name (with the two titles intentionally sounding similar). But *Best Runs* differs in three other ways: The material is all new (no piece appeared in the earlier book), it's more personal in tone (I intend for you to see yourself in the stories written about myself), and it's less about running farther and faster than about having the best possible running experiences.

Best Runs passed through editing as I celebrated my 40th anniversary as a runner. This book tells of ways to make running last longest, and that final *-est* word ultimately means the most. Times may slow, distances may shrink, old glories may fade. But the running itself goes on. I plan to run into the indefinite future and hope you'll go along with me. Some of our best days lie ahead.

Joe Henderson

PART

I

Best Ways

1

Picking the Best Bets

Best is a slippery concept in running. The search for the best running systems is endless because what's best for one person doesn't necessarily transfer for another, and what's best for you today might not work later as your goals change.

FIFTY IS NIFTY

You're never too old or too experienced to learn (or relearn) running tricks. I'll shower you with tips in this opening chapter, then we'll return later for longer looks at these lessons. We start with a personal review I conducted a few years ago. This wasn't just any day, but my birthday. It wasn't just any birthday either, but my 50th.

Talk about ominous beginnings to a new half-century. I woke up shortly after midnight with a cold taking a stranglehold on my throat. No run this day. A few hours later I flipped on my computer to start the day's writing and the screen stayed dark. The power had failed.

The morning-starting cup of hot tea went to work on my throat. A new power line to my office replaced the one that shorted out. I was ready to contemplate my half-century on this planet.

Turning 50 meant more than just reaching another calendar page. It was a milepost that caused me to look back at the last decade marker and to judge how far I'd traveled since then. You don't see this from one day to the next, or even from one year to another. Only a more distant view can bring the details of the journey into focus.

I was a better runner than on the last birthday that ended with a zero. Slower, yes, but only the watch signals any such decline. Otherwise I was better in health, better in energy, and better in overall fitness at 50 than at 40.

My running had slipped into a rut during my late 30s. The boundaries of my racing had shrunk to little more than 5Ks to 10Ks. I'd retired from miles and marathons. I ran the same short, slow, steady half-hours daily. And I mean every day, in streaks that lasted as long as five years without a rest.

At age 40 I always ran in the same pair of shoes. I never did anything but run. I neglected my upper body, inside and out. My diet was haphazard, and my weight, cholesterol, and blood pressure had crept up. My arms and stomach muscles had shriveled from lack of activity.

During my 40s the running became more varied and the fitness better balanced. I wasn't too old or too experienced to learn (or relearn) these tricks:

- **Big day.** Replaced one of the week's all-easy runs with a harder one, going longer or faster, or longer and faster, than in a race.

- **Shorter races.** Raced as short as a mile, and back on the track, for the first time since my 20s.

- **Longer races.** Raced as long as a marathon, after nearly 10 years of "retirement" from this event.

- **Shorter and faster runs.** Added a 1-1-1 plan to my training— one mile, one minute faster than normal training pace, once a week.

- **Longer and slower runs.** Added frequent runs longer than one hour with a one-minute walk-break option.

- **Rest days.** Started taking one day off each week, or more often if health conditions required resting.

- **Shoe changes.** No longer wore the same pair of shoes two days in a row; rotated several pairs.

- **Lower-fat diet.** Cut the intake in half, which led to positive reversals in weight, cholesterol, and blood-pressure trends.

- **Upper-body exercise.** Adopted small but regular amount of weight training to put a little meat back on these old bones and perhaps strengthen the bones as well.

- **Lower-body alternatives.** Took on hiking, biking, and water running as substitutes when running wasn't possible or advisable.

At 40 I still worried that any run not taken would be lost forever. But at 50 I was willing to skip a run today to make tomorrow's better. I wouldn't have considered resting a cold on my 40th birthday. I wouldn't consider running with a cold on my 50th. That's progress.

TIME TRIALS

Best is a slippery concept in running. The search for the best running systems is endless because what's best for one person doesn't necessarily transfer for another, and what's best for you today might not work later as your goals change.

I've spent lots of years searching for better ways to run and writing about them. Back in 1967, the year when running writing became my full-time work, I thought there was little left to learn about the sport. Now had come my time to teach. Yet the learning continued. It still does, and may it never stop. Every item on the list of 20 below—which previews much of what fills this book—joined it after 1967. Some lessons span that entire period, while others are of recent coinage.

These aren't philosophical generalities like "Everyone's a winner" or "There is no finish line." They aren't trivial personal quirks like going sockless in winter or taking showers before races. These are specific tricks that have direct, measurable effects on running performance and enjoyment. I'm slower—okay, much slower—than I was in the 1960s. But I'm also measurably healthier and happier for the added experience.

© Ken Lee

These schemes have caught on with me. You may have seen them dribble across magazine and newsletter pages, and into previous books. I introduced a few of them in the opening section of this chapter and don't hesitate to re-emphasize them here because they cut to the core of the advice I give and the running I practice.

Some of the ideas will sound weird to you. The only defense is that they've stood up to years of self-testing. There are no guarantees they will work for you. Only your own time trials can tell you that.

WEIRD IDEAS THAT WORK

1. Seldom push the distance or the pace. Run between a half-hour and an hour most days. Set the effort at "comfortable," whatever that might mean that day or at that moment.

2. Count no miles outside of races. Run by time periods, not by distance. Break free from measured courses and the pressure to break records on them.

3. Plan the run after starting. Prerun feelings often lie. Wait to see how running really feels until the first 10 minutes has shaken out kinks, doubts, and delusions.

4. Heed warning signs. Give in to pains that interfere with normal running form, fail to ease during the warm-up minutes, or grow worse as the run goes on. Stop now and try again tomorrow.

5. Take walks in long runs. Insert 1-minute walking breaks at about 10-minute intervals to shake off temporary aches, to speed recovery from races and injuries, and to exceed normal distance limits.

6. Take no penalty for days off. Replace weekly or monthly running totals with daily averages. Count only run days, not rest days, in that average.

7. Limit the racing. Choose one of these limitations: 10 percent of the month's running, one easy day per kilometer raced, or one easy week per hour raced.

8. Save the biggest efforts for races. In occasional training runs go long but slowly or fast but briefly. Only go long and fast in the races, where it counts.

9. Use races as training. Build racing speed by running short races, of less than an hour. Build racing endurance only in the long races, lasting more than an hour.

10. Set minimum racing goals: just to finish, or to run "at least" so fast. Let exceeding that baseline come as a surprise, not as an expectation.

11. Warm up little if any for races: little for short ones, none for those lasting longer than an hour. Use the early race as a warm-up to guard against starting too fast.

12. Race like a vulture. Cruise along in the first half, letting the early flyers do their passing. Pass up the dead and dying in the last half when it means something.

13. Believe in magic. Trust the raceday excitement to give a minute-per-mile bonus in pace versus running the same distance alone, or to double the distance a pace can be held solo.

14. Stretch after running, not before. Stretch when the muscles need it most and are warmest. Warm up for running by running, and treat stretching as a preventive-maintenance exercise to ease postrun tightness.

15. Carbo-load during and after running, not before. Take the legal drug of sugar (from energy gel or bar packets) during the longest runs to extend endurance, and carbo-reload soon afterward to speed recovery.

Arthur Lydiard

I owe much to this New Zealander for my training ideas. I've edited his methods almost beyond recognition to serve my purposes, yet his early influence remains. This tribute to him appeared in the March 1997 *Running Commentary,* as he neared his 80th birthday.

No one made a bigger or longer-lasting contribution to running training than Lydiard. In 1960, most of the athletic world had barely even heard of New Zealand, a South Pacific island nation with a population of 3 million. Then at the Rome Olympics, the New Zealanders defied all predictions by winning two gold medals and a bronze in the distance runs. All three runners—Peter Snell, Murray Halberg, and Barrie Magee—came from the same neighborhood in Auckland. All were coached by Lydiard. They soon were breaking world records, and Snell would win twice at the Tokyo games.

Lydiard had parted with conventional wisdom of the day, which dictated intense year-round interval training on the track. His athletes trained on long-distance work in the off-season, then gradually honed themselves to a sharp peak with steadily faster training. He revolutionized running training worldwide.

The New Zealand success was repeated when Lydiard coached in Mexico and in Finland. His message was widely spread and well received in the United States, thanks to help from his "disciple" Bill Bowerman. Lydiard's methods often were misinterpreted, however. And Lydiard himself (who was a shoemaker by profession, not a scientifically trained coach) wasn't totally clear on why his system worked. At least he never explained it in *Run to the Top* or his later books, which now are decades old and out of print. Much of what he taught is now either misused or forgotten. This is a shame, says Dick Brown, who has studied training methods his entire career and recently discovered Lydiard.

The Lydiard principles still apply, more than 35 years after he first outlined them, says Brown. In fact, he adds, "No subsequent method has improved significantly on them." Brown is a brilliant coach in his own right. He has sent athletes to the Olympics in distance running, race walking and cross-country skiing, as well as swimming in the Paralympics. His greatest tribute to the master is that his own training of runners and others is increasingly Lydiard-based. (Shortly after this article appeared, Arthur Lydiard published a new book titled *Running to the Top*, from the German publisher Meyer & Meyer Verlag.)

BEST ANSWERS

Maybe all training advice should come with a warning label. It need not go so far as to say, "Caution: This program may be hazardous to your health, or at least to your peace of mind." But it might say, "There are many different ways to train, so you'll read lots of conflicting advice."

Hal Higdon, senior writer for *Runner's World* magazine, addressed this problem in an article. "Training can get awfully confusing," he admitted at the top. "So much has been said and written about how to train, what to eat, where to run. There are, it seems, a zillion ways to do speedwork, scores of stretches and dozens of shoe models."

The magazines and books hand you a menu offering many different entrees. All the recipes presumably have passed someone's tests. But you're still left to select those that best suit your needs and tastes, and this is where the confusion lies.

Higdon did the ordering for his readers. He selected a single best method or product in several categories. Hal has hung around the sport longer than any of the *RW* writers. After 50 years of running he's certain of what is best for him. But even he can't say that all runners will like his selections. There is no one best answer that satisfies everyone, only a best one for you.

Like Hal Higdon, I've made my choices. Consider his and mine to be fill-in-the-blank order forms. We've completed ours (for now, but reserve the right to change). After reading my answers below, decide where yours agree and differ.

- Best normal daily run: A gentle half-hour, which is enough to feel like I've done something worthwhile but not so much that I can't do it again the next day.

- Best longer run: One hour, which is double the norm and the point where long runs begin for me.

- Best spacing of longer runs: Once every week or two.

- Best longest run: Two hours, which is my minimum for marathon foundation laying.

- Best spacing of longest runs: Monthly, or slightly more often if training for a marathon.

- Best faster run: One mile at about 10K race pace, preceded by a half-hour warm-up.

- Best spacing of faster runs: Once every week or two.

- Best easy day: The easiest of all and the quickest way to recover-rest.

- Best combination of running and rest: Hard day (long or fast training run, or race), then easy (rest or gentle run) for the next two or more days.

- Best short race: 5K, where the pace is the fastest I'm prepared to run.

- Best long race: Half-marathon, where real racing ends for me and survival-running begins.

- Best rest after racing: One day for short races, and one day per hour of the long races, before running again at all.

- Best wait before racing again: One day for each kilometer of the last race.

- Best supplemental exercise: Walking, taken as short breaks in midrun, as warm-up or cool-down, or as a substitute for running.

- Best use of walks in long runs or marathons: One minute of walking in every 10 minutes of running (or about a minute per mile), on average.

- Best time for stretching: Right after the run, incorporated into the cool-down.

- Best strength exercise: Barbell presses for the otherwise-neglected upper body.

- Best prerace meal: Nothing solid before morning races except perhaps an energy bar.

- Best food during an extra-long race or run of two hours or more: One of the gels.

- Best drink immediately before, during, and after races: Plain water.

- Best shoe: A light, cushiony, low-end model with price to match.

- Best socks: None, in any weather.

- Best watch: A cheap and simple digital, suitable for technophobes like me.

- Best time of day: Sunrise, when the air is coolest and cleanest.

- Best day of the week: Sunday, when traffic is lightest and my time is freest.

- Best season of the year: Fall, which recalls cross-country seasons of my youth.

- Best place to run: The sawdust cross-country trails of Eugene, Oregon, which begin less than a mile from home.

2

Training by the Numbers

The first half-hour is a warm-up, a fitness run, and a test of ability to do more. This you do for the body. What follows is self-indulgence. The first half-hour undoubtedly makes good exercise, but exercising is just a stage to pass through to get to the better part. That overtime period makes running worth doing and keeps you coming back for more.

START WITH COOPER

Kenneth Cooper, MD, influenced you, whether you know his name and read his books or not. Dr. Cooper had more to do with making running what it is today than any other American. Cooper invented Aerobics with a capital "A." He showed me in 1968, in his first book, that running was more than a sport. It could also be an exercise, one that would bring thousands of nonathletes into this activity.

He had it right then and still does—as far as he goes. The only problem with his advice is that he would have us stop where most of us are just getting started.

Cooper once wrote a line I've repeated dozens of times—then added a qualifier of my own. After he recommended two- to three-mile runs, three to five days a week, he said, "If you run more than 15 miles a week, you're doing it for reasons other than fitness." He could point to a million research subjects to support this claim. He could show that fitness gains dwindle and injury rates soar after the 15-mile mark.

I can't argue with his research. He's no doubt right—as far as he goes. But I add that there are great reasons to run other than fitness. Or I should say, in addition to fitness.

Another great doctor explained this best. "Fitness is a stage you pass through on the way to becoming a runner," said George Sheehan, MD. Recreation, relaxation, and competition are a few of those reasons to keep going. All of these start at a point where Dr. Cooper would ask us to stop. And all involve some degree of risk, happily taken.

I've never wanted to stop after three miles, but it seems a smart place to start. Cooper is right that we must take care of the body first, and the best way to do this is his way. I never count miles, but the doctor himself would approve of the 30 minutes that I run five days of most weeks. At current stiff-legged opening pace, that time is worth just a tad more than three miles.

But I don't stop here. My homage to Cooper ends at the half-hour, five days a week. On the sixth day, the week's Big Day, I get to meet George Sheehan's definition of a runner. On this day I warm up the Cooper way . . . then add at least another half-hour of running . . . or add a mile or more at a much faster pace . . . or run both farther and faster than normal in a race.

The Cooper opening is a warm-up, a fitness run, and a test of ability to do more that day or later that week. This you do for the body. What follows is self-indulgence. The first half-hour undoubtedly is good exercise, but exercising is just a stage to pass through to get to the better part. That overtime period on the Big Day makes running worth doing and keeps you coming back for more.

TWICE AS NICE

Running theorists often talk of quantity and quality as opposites. The first has to do with amount and the second with intensity, they say, and you must place your emphasis on one or the other. Quality training involves running fewer miles, faster. I disagree with this

© Ken Lee

definition. Running can lose quality as the amount drops and gain quality as it increases, regardless of its intensity.

The biggest and best change of my running life came in 1966 when I dropped out of intense, track-based training in favor of gentler running on the roads. The second-best came about 20 years later when I dropped out of everyday running in favor of longer runs, taken less often.

Starting in 1966, I ran an hour on more days than not. The longer and shorter runs offset each other to yield a daily average right at one hour. I could get away with this much as a young-legged runner in my 20s and 30s. Then my recovery rate slowed with age, as tends to happen with most runners.

By my 40s the average run had eroded badly. I still ran daily—insisted on it, in fact, while protecting a years-long streak of running days—but now barely went a half-hour at a time. I wanted more from running than easy halves. This was enough for fitness, maybe, but not enough to give what I'd come to expect from running. These runs ended too soon, before letting me know I'd done anything worthwhile.

I could run the half-hour in my sleep, and many mornings almost did. The run ended before the good part started, and I needed that second half-hour back. But how to reclaim it? Short as the runs were then, I still didn't recover well from one day to the next. Low-grade soreness and tiredness were chronic, and running more each day would only have aggravated those symptoms.

I turned to running's adviser in chief, George Sheehan, for help. What he said wasn't so much advice as permission to do what I knew had to be done but had resisted doing. "I never used to take days off either," said George. "Then I realized this was detracting from what I really wanted to accomplish as a runner."

George was first a racer and wasn't racing as well as he liked. He didn't recover enough from one race to the next. He took one day off a week, and his racing improved. He took two rest days a week and improved even more. He finally settled into an every-other-day program.

"I run the same total amount each week as I did before," he said at the time. "I simply distribute it differently by running twice as much, half as often." He added that the runs taken were fewer but far more satisfying than before.

I haven't yet gotten down to George's every-other-day plan, or up

Fred Wilt

The words you now read descended directly from Wilt's early advice. He told me to keep a running diary, which began immediately, became training for all the writing that followed, and remains a daily habit today. *Running Commentary* in October 1994 carried this article when he died at age 73.

Fred Wilt's work pulled American distance runners out of the Dark Ages. As a runner who finished 11th and 21st in his Olympic 10,000s, he set out to learn what the world's best runners knew and his countrymen didn't. This research grew into the *Track & Field News* book, *How They Train*, which literally reproduced dozens of training programs. The Golden Age of U.S. running began soon afterward.

Wilt's first book led to another, titled *Run-Run-Run*. By then he was gathering enough material to fill the quarterly journal, *Track Technique* (which Wilt originally edited and *Track & Field News* still publishes under the name *Track Coach*). All this from someone who hadn't trained to be a writer or a coach.

He served a full career as an agent in J. Edgar Hoover's FBI and coached only incidentally during most of those years. The little coaching Wilt did was as unusual as it was successful. Buddy Edelen lived in England, and Wilt's coaching came entirely by mail from Indiana. In 1963, Edelen became the first American in more than half a century to set a world marathon record with 2:14:28. Hal Higdon, now one of the sport's best-known writers, enlisted Wilt as his own coach-by-mail in 1963. They pointed Hal's training toward the 1964 Boston Marathon, where he ran a PR of 2:21:55, placed fifth, and led all Americans.

Wilt turned to formal, full-time coaching only after leaving the FBI. He had a long second career as coach of the women's team at Purdue University before retiring in 1990.

The day a brief notice of Wilt's death appeared in my local newspaper, I called Hal Higdon right away. "I wish I had made a greater effort to see Fred in recent years," said Hal that morning. "It was just a phone call now and then. Ironically, I had planned to call him today." He could have asked his question of anyone in his world of contacts. Hal paid his old coach a final compliment by thinking Fred Wilt's answer would be the best.

to his hour-a-day average. I'm too fond of running to run that seldom. But I thank him for giving me the okay to take the rest I needed. The days off made me more of a runner again on the "on" days. The running is better for it.

BALANCING ACT

He walked up to me after a talk in Chicago and made a bold request for such a shy-acting man. Stewart Sims said, "I'm writing a book about running and wonder if you'll write a chapter for me." I have enough writing of my own to do without helping anyone else, but Stewart asked so nicely that I couldn't refuse him.

My plan was to recycle something already written, but he had other plans: "Would you summarize the talk you gave in Chicago?" It was the talk I'd been giving, with little evolutionary change, for the past decade or more. Strangely, though, I'd never written it all down.

Typing it took only about an hour. That's at least triple my normal writing pace. No surprise here. I've had 10 years of practice at talking out this piece titled "Farther, Faster, Fresher." It began:

> Ask me for one word to introduce myself and I won't choose *writer* or *author*. Even the word *runner* is inadequate. I prefer to think of myself as *survivor*. I'm nearing the 40th anniversary of my running—which began on an April Fool's Day 1958. This timing might be fitting, since I've made every dumb mistake known to the sport.
>
> And yet I've survived to tell about it. I never call myself *just a survivor,* as if this were a consolation prize. I've come to realize that survival is the highest calling of a runner. Few of us ever win any prize of note, and those prizes soon tarnish and gather dust. Press clippings, if we're lucky enough to earn such attention, eventually yellow and crumble. Pace eventually and inevitably slows. All that lasts is the running itself—the wanting to and being able to get up and do it all over again each day.

I write and speak in praise of keeping going, as someone who has done that. We might not have the talent to outrun other runners, but we all can gain the skills and smarts to outlast them.

Survival as a runner is a balancing act among the three factors. In daily phone calls and letters, and in all my travels, I hear the following posed as questions:

1. "How can I run farther?" Someone trying a first marathon usually asks this question, but it can come from anyone taking a major upward step in distance.

2. "How can I run faster?" This is the question from someone who has run some 5 and 10Ks just to finish and now wants to set PRs.

3. "How can I get over the problems I'm having from running farther and faster?" I hear this from runners who have overdone the first two factors while ignoring the vital third, which is recovery between the long and fast runs.

FAR, FAST, FRESH

In the section that follows I offer some answers to the questions of how long, how fast, how easy. These formulas may sound simple (and even simplistic). But realize that behind each lies years of blood, sweat, and tears from their originators. The formulas might not fit you perfectly. But at least they'll point you toward possible solutions to your running imbalances.

Running Fresher

I switch the order here, starting with what not to run, because it's the least exciting and perhaps most important. Different formulas apply here to racing and to training.

Racing is exciting to think about and challenging to do. But it's also a taxing act in which you can't indulge too often. How often? The best advice I ever read came from Jack Foster, a New Zealander who ran a 2:11 marathon at age 41. That time stood as a world masters record for 16 years.

Foster realized that runners don't necessarily slow down by the watch with age, but their recovery rates do slow. He allowed himself one day of recovery for each mile of the race—a week after a 10K, for instance, or a month after a marathon. Recovery, Foster-style, doesn't mean total rest, but it does mean no runs longer than one hour, no speedwork, and certainly no further racing during that risky postrace period. If you have trouble recovering from race to race, consider the Foster formula.

If you have trouble simply recovering from day-to-day runs, consider taking more days off. Rest at least one day a week, if not drop to every-other-day running as George Sheehan did. In his midlife he became a spokesman for rest (as explained earlier in this chapter). George set his marathon PR at age 60, while resting three or even four days each week. Rest, he had discovered, is the key to making the hard work work.

Running Farther

Olympian-turned-writer Jeff Galloway revolutionized marathon training, and therefore brought this distance within reach of thousands more runners. Galloway's main contributions were two.

First, he took the emphasis away from adding up high mileage each week, which didn't allow runners enough easy or rest days because they feared a loss of miles. Galloway shifted the emphasis to longer long runs, with more recovery time in between than runners had allowed themselves previously. The longest training runs approached marathon length, but no longer came around

weekly but only every two or three weeks. This allowed the runner to take the most important run eagerly and energetically instead of with a sense of weary dread.

If you have trouble recovering from one long run to the next, consider the Galloway formula of putting more R&R in between. This works for any longer running, not just marathon training. If you have trouble just finishing long runs, consider a second innovation that Galloway popularized. That is to insert walking breaks into the long runs.

Jeff adopted and adapted this practice from ultramarathoner Tom Osler. In his *Serious Runner's Handbook*, Osler says, "You can instantly double the length of your longest nonstop run by adding walking breaks." A common application of this technique is to take a one-minute walk after each mile of running.

Running Faster

The most common malady among today's runners isn't Achilles tendinitis or shinsplints. It's the one-pace-runner syndrome. Runners never suffered this way in the dark ages. Back then, long before running boomed, we ran fast from day one. This system took a high toll in injuries and burnout. But it did teach us how to run fast, which is a skill like swimming or bicycling. Once you learn it, your body never forgets it.

Most of today's runners began differently, which is to say the right way for getting fit sensibly. First they walked or ran slowly, then gradually upped the amount of running. They developed a low, short, efficient stride. This served them well for covering long distances—but not well for going fast. They'd never learned how to shift into a higher gear. So their pace was the same for training and racing, for 5K and 10K and half-marathon. (Walt Stack, a legend in San Francisco running, once complained, "If they dropped me out of an airplane, I would fall at $8\frac{1}{2}$ minutes per mile.")

Running faster can be as simple as the 1-1-1 plan put forth by Dick Buerkle. This two-time Olympian and former world-indoor-record holder in the mile scaled down his speed training into a simple workout: One mile, one day a week, one minute faster than normal pace. For instance, a runner stuck at 8:30 per mile would warm up, then run the mile on a track or other flat, measured course in about 7:30. Speeding up once a week this way can lead to improvements of 10 or 20 seconds a mile, and even more, in races.

If you have trouble speeding up, consider this addition to your plan. The payoff for this one mile a week can be a one-minute improvement, or more, per 10K.

3

Learning How to Walk

Walk breaks bring the marathon within reach of thousands more entrants. The breakers contribute heavily to the current robust health of the event, which is now the biggest—and slowest—in its history.

WALK TALK

If you're a purist who fears that the gods of running will throw down a lightning bolt and strike you dead if you ever take so much as one walking step during a run, fear not. This isn't a sinful practice but a productive one.

Walking for runners is one of my favorite themes—if not a crusade. But it wasn't always this way. Once I was a purist, as were most runners in the Dark Ages. We ran in circles at stoplights to avoid this fate. We'd toss drinks in our faces or over our shoulders rather than stop at aid stations.

My first brush with the idea of walking breaks came in the 1960s by way of Ernst Van Aaken, a German physician-coach. He called this the "natural" way to train and recommended it for everyone from beginners to world-class athletes. Weird, I thought. Real runners don't take walks.

Then in 1970 I wrote a story about British adventurer Kenneth Crutchlow. He'd just run between Los Angeles and San Francisco. "Anyone could do this if he trained," said Crutchlow. "The challenge is to do it without training." His trick was to run a mile or so, then walk, then run some more. "It took me the whole bloody day," he said, "but I did my 50 miles a day for 10 days straight."

This intrigued me enough to try it in a 100-mile race. I ran and walked 70 miles of the race—which was a failure for being a nonfinish but an eye-opener in other senses: The 70-mile distance was more than twice as far as I'd ever gone nonstop, my running pace was just a half-minute per mile slower than my marathons, and my recovery was much faster than after any marathon. I stored this away in the "interesting but impractical" file. I would soon undergo surgery that would forever limit mileage, block trying another ultra, and make marathons risky.

In 1978 Tom Osler brought this technique into the real world (or at least the one I inhabited by then). He wrote in *Runner's World*, and later in the classic *Serious Runner's Handbook*, that walking breaks worked for ultrarunners like himself, but also for people trying to make the jump between half-marathons and marathons, 10Ks and halves. He was the first to put this into a formula: Run 5 to 25 minutes (depending on ability) and walk 5 minutes.

By then I was semiretired from marathons. I thought: I've run them with too much training, just enough, and too little. Why not

Tom Osler

Osler is one of running's unsung geniuses—a genius because of what he wrote in the modern sport's formative years. And unsung because he never opted to become a star in print and on stage. Here's what I wrote about him in the March 1998 *Running Commentary.*

Tom Osler prefers to be known as a mathematics professor. He teaches and researches the subject at Rowan University in New Jersey. His running writing is almost 20 years behind him, but its influence lives on even if he doesn't get or seek credit. He is, for instance, the father of the now-popular walking breaks, though he isn't and wouldn't care to be known as such.

The slim booklet *Conditioning of Distance Runners,* published in the mid-1960s by *Long Distance Log,* laid the foundation for bigger and better-known books to follow. None was better, then or since, than his own *Serious Runner's Handbook* (World Publications). It contains more than 300 gems of simple wisdom. Tom doesn't toy with a piece of advice for a chapter when he can dispose of it in a paragraph.

We recently caught up on our years out of touch with each other. He talked first about family and then his work. "My deepest interest at the moment is in mathematical research," he said. Tom put his running in its proper place, talking about it only third. He doesn't write about the sport anymore but still lives it. "I now run much less and much slower," said the 57-year-old former ultrarunner. "I have not run an ultra since 1982 due to foot problems. I now run about 20 miles per week in the winter and 50 in the summer."

The math man is proudest now of his own cumulative numbers: "I am now in my 44th consecutive year of running and have completed more than 1550 races. I can't run fast anymore, but I can keep adding to the years of running and the list of races. It's kind of an old man's marathon."

A trace of regret shows when he says, "There was a time when I could coast through 50 consecutive 7-minute miles. Now I am straining after *two* 7-minute miles. I miss being able to go out the door and run endlessly with no effort. I only have memories of such effortless joy. But, oh, what memories!"

run one with no training—nothing long, that is? My longest run that fall had been six miles. Using Oslerian breaks in my next marathon, I ran a PW—personal worst—but not by nearly the margin expected and with less effort than feared.

Again this technique went on the shelf for me. I "retired" from marathons for almost a decade and just wrote about them, mentioning walking breaks whenever possible.

Marathoning's second boom, which began around 1990, was too exciting to miss. I'm back on a modest one- or two-marathons-a-year pace while training minimally long. I wouldn't dare attempt the full distance without great faith in the walks. They've never let me down.

Sure, my marathons are an hour slower than before. But the point is, I wouldn't be finishing them at any pace without the walks. My practice has settled at walking an average of 1 minute in 10, or about a minute per mile. The breaks can come every mile, or lumped two or three together for an equal number of miles.

This one-minute pause is what Jeff Galloway and I arrived at independently of each other (see chapter 2). He advises thousands of marathoners, and most of them walk early and often, for about a minute at a time. When I run marathons and see people slam on their brakes after the first mile, it's easy to guess whose advice they're following. Thanks to Jeff's missionary work, the weirdness has gone out of walking.

WALK WARS

Way back when, we fought holy wars over running pace. On one side of this battle line stood the old guard, who believed it wasn't really training if it wasn't fast enough to hurt. Lining up on the other side were the rebels who practiced and promoted the ambling, long, slow distance (LSD) style of running. The traditionalists shouted that the LSDers were undercutting serious running, blaming them for a decline in U.S. racing performances. The LSDers countered that the speed killed the legs and spirit of its practitioners.

These two groups finally agreed to coexist in relative peace. Anyway, nearly everyone came to practice some slow running, even runners who won't stoop to calling it "LSD."

While peace has broken out on this front, a new holy war appears to be brewing. It too has to do with pace and effort, now pitting run-every-step runners against the growing run-with-walk-breaks crowd.

I paid a yearly visit to the Portland Marathon Clinic's training group and noticed its healthy numbers. I mentioned this to the director of another marathon. "But do they run the distance," he asked, "or do they take those walking breaks?" The trend away from marathon-as-race and toward marathon-as-survival-test bothered him. "Maybe we give these people certificates of under-achievement," he said. "I'm from the old school that believes the marathon is a running event."

He's far from alone. I've heard many such thoughts, usually privately expressed as this race director's were, that the walkers somehow cheapen the sport and don't really belong in the company of pure runners.

Reports reached me about a certain leader of a marathon training group who targeted Jeff Galloway, the best-known point man for planned walks during long runs and races. The critic told his group that a marathon finish "doesn't count if you don't run all the way." My spies took down his descriptions of walking breaks as "an unproven method" and a "marketing ploy."

Come, now. This isn't religion or politics. To walk or not to walk isn't a serious enough matter to cause verbal bloodshed, just as LSD versus speed wasn't a big enough subject to divide us into warring camps.

LSD once brought long-distance running within reach of thousands more runners, making the sport bigger and better for those who chose to keep running hard and fast. The invasion of LSDers had the side benefit of making the serious folks feel faster than they had before without even upping their pace. Now the walk breaks bring the marathon within reach of thousands more entrants. The breakers contribute heavily to the current robust health of the event, which is now the biggest—and slowest—in its history. They make the pure runners look faster without having to work any harder.

If you believe that a marathon is only a run, then don't walk. But don't deny these breaks to the marathoners who can't or won't go this far without them.

STOPPING AND DRINKING

Natasha Perry is a marathoner today because she was willing to walk. After becoming one, she sent me a letter that began with a thank you, in boldface type and followed by six exclamation points. "I used the book you wrote, *Marathon Training*, and I am happy to say that it was a success."

She'd never run longer than 10 miles before picking up the book. It somehow made going $2\frac{1}{2}$ times that far sound possible. Natasha, then 27, chose the "cruiser" program for people whose goal is to finish. This plan encourages them to insert walking breaks. She didn't take them as early as prescribed, but waited until 15 miles to begin the minute-per-mile walks. The result: "I finished in 4:12:30, but I can't say that I wasn't in agony those last six miles as my legs screamed ferociously with each push."

Her only criticism of the book: no advice on drinking during long training runs and the marathon itself. "As a novice," she said,

"I did not realize how much I needed to have water along with me and to be sure to drink plenty before I even started the runs. It was, however, a lesson that I quickly learned on my first 15-mile run, and consequently I never made the same mistake again."

The letter ended with another thanks: "You have created a cruiser marathoner." My reply began with "Bravo" (and a single exclamation point).

Then I said: "You give me some of the credit for your triumph, but I deserve very little. I just wrote the book. You did all the work of bringing the program to life, and now earn all the praise.

"You're right, the book needed advice on drinking. The next book (this one) will make up for that oversight, since I now realize that, like many runners, I've labored along chronically dehydrated. Now I both practice and preach what you've already learned: Stop at every water station, or carry your own bottle(s).

"Your final 10K might have been less of a struggle if you hadn't waited until 15 miles to start the walking breaks. They're most effective when taken early, starting in the first few miles. I prefer taking a minute's break from the first milepost on, but because of crowding and excitement usually wait until 20 or 30 minutes into the event. An alternate plan is to walk for a minute or two at each drink stop, where lots of other people are already walking. These usually appear at least every two miles.

"You wouldn't want to wait to drink until you're really thirsty. Likewise you don't want to wait to walk until you're really tired. Early drinking keeps you from becoming too thirsty. Early walking keeps you from becoming too tired."

WALKING LESSONS

Walking lessons? You might as well take eating or breathing lessons. Isn't walking a skill we learn around the age of one and then never forget? Not really. Children don't stand up and walk. Their first steps are lunging runs into the arms of waiting parents. They don't slow down much until their teenage years, then soon get a driver's license and thereafter limit their walking to crossing parking lots.

A few of us keep running after learning to drive. I was among the lucky ones. But almost 20 years passed after my first formal race before I finally learned to walk. That is, how to stop and walk

29

during a run to ease the pain or extend the distance. Or to take a walk some days instead of running at all.

I've written about the whys and whens of walking. Now I want to deal with some whos. These walking lessons came by mail. One writer is from the best possible source, the other a surprising one. The first is Ron Laird, who made four Olympic teams as a race walker. The second is Richard Leutzinger, a man I always saw as a pure runner.

Ron sent his book, *The Art of Fast Walking*. He directed a chapter of the book, and a paragraph in his cover letter, to runners. "For years," he told me in the letter, "I have felt it safer and more sensible for people to build their fitness with faster walking before attempting slower training. We both know that race walking can get pretty crazy at the international level, with its rules and disqualifications. However, when slowed down to a 10- to 12-minute-per-mile pace I feel that race walking is the safest, healthiest, and most convenient physical fitness activity ever invented."

I can't argue any of those points. At seven minutes a mile, most race walkers appear to the untrained eye to be running. But I'm sure that Ron's right that at a slower pace where rules become irrelevant, the benefits are great and the risks small.

Richard Leutzinger surprised me by agreeing—at least with the general point of selective walking helping runners. He once shared the trails of Pebble Beach, California, with me. We never ran together there, though, because his pace was several gears above mine.

He was trained as a journalist. Although he now works in health care, the urge to write stays with him. He penned a book about baseball player Lefty O'Doul, then counted dozens of rejections before finding a publishing house to take the book. Such endurance also serves him well as a runner. In his late 50s he still ran marathons in the low threes and contended for age-group prizes.

"I've run 52 marathons now and have never learned to drink on the run—probably because I've never tried," Richard said in a letter. "I've always felt that the time I lost while stopping to drink 5-6-7-8 times benefited me, so it wasn't time 'lost' at all. Those little walk breaks are really refreshing, physically and mentally. I determine whether I'm hydrated by whether I have to make any stops to pee, and whether my forehead feels dry or sweaty. If I'm well hydrated at 20 miles, I might consider passing up the last few drink stops—unless I just need that little break from running."

An aid station is the ideal spot to stop for another reason besides the one Richard notes. So many people are already walking there anyway, and the break-taking is less obvious. (A plea to walkers: Look before you stop, or a runner could rear-end you. Better yet, pull to the curb or sidewalk, out of traffic flow. I like to walk behind the drink tables.)

Richard also reported taking breaks of as long as 15 minutes in training, while indulging in his hobby of collecting stray golf balls on the Pebble Beach courses. This new wrinkle in his routine hadn't hurt his racing.

"This fall I ran my fastest marathon in nearly four years," he said of his recent 3:15. "So I guess the system works okay."

4

Running Out of Time

Our sport is custom-made for hurriers. It always holds

up times to beat and deadlines to meet. But if time is

the cause of hurry sickness, it can also supply the

cure. We can work at relaxing by making friends

with the clock.

SHOUTING SOFTLY

Bert Nelson, one of the sport's all-time great writers, penned one of the greatest lines. The *Track & Field News* cofounder compared race walking to "seeing who can whisper the loudest." Fast walkers fight the natural urge to break into a run. Why else would that sport need judges?

Slow running is equally odd for the opposite reason. It seems to go against the whole purpose of running, which is to move swiftly. The natural urge when slowing a run is to fall into a walk. Reversing the Nelson line, running slowly is like seeing who can shout most softly. While acknowledging its quirk, I've long praised slow running. A better term for it might be relaxed running at any speed.

I'm not opposed to going fast as such. Hundreds of times in races and thousands in practice, I've run as fast as possible. Many of my stories lionize the athletes who go fastest of all. What I'm against is a chronic, harried sense of urgency in all runs—especially when it spills over into a headlong rush through all of life. This is treating the clock as a constant enemy to be subdued. It's trying to finish every 10-minute job in 5 minutes.

Meyer Friedman, MD, coined the phrase *Type-A personality*. He identified its main symptom as *hurry sickness*. Friedman listed its traits as "excessive competitive drive, aggressiveness, impatience, and a harrying sense of time urgency. Individuals displaying this pattern seem to be engaged in chronic, ceaseless, and often fruitless struggle—with themselves, with others, with circumstances, with time, sometimes with life itself."

Runners are particularly susceptible, because our sport is custom-made for hurriers. It always holds up times to beat and deadlines to meet. But if time is the cause of hurry sickness, it can also supply the cure. We can work at relaxing by making friends with the clock.

One of the best changes I ever made to my running was switching to the time standard. I quit counting miles and simply ran for, say, an hour without knowing the distance covered. I began running this way for practical reasons: not wanting to measure all courses and never wanting to stray from these routes. I soon found a better reason to run by time: relief from rushing. Our natural urge when running by miles is to finish them as quickly as possible.

Running by minutes, which can't be rushed, we naturally adopt an unhurried pace.

Another problem can remain, even with time-running. That's scheduling the running time too tightly—rushing to get started, hurrying away afterward, and canceling the calming effect of the run itself. The cure: Take more time than needed. Provide a relaxed buffer period on either side of the run.

I set aside twice as much time as the run takes—allowing two hours total for a one-hour run, for instance. This gives me unpressured time to get ready for the run and to recover afterward.

I've made friends with the clock these same ways in writing, where time is also a primary raw material and where I like to "shout softly." Each essay in this book took only about two hours to write, but I fit that time loosely into half a day. This let me write with a relaxed pace and tone, and left equally important space in the margins for unhurried planning and reflecting.

An old boss of mine, being a businessman editor himself, didn't appreciate the time requirements of writers. He said, "You waste too much time staring out the window." This time isn't wasted. Writers and runners alike need as many hours for sitting silently as for shouting softly.

HONEST EFFORTS

By the standards of runners at large, my efforts are all rather puny. But I try to be honest about them—with you, yes, but especially with myself. Most of my efforts can only be called "easy." The two main sources of excitement and trouble in my past running—races and extra-long training runs that mimic the racing effort—have all but disappeared.

I now race—really race and not just run along in races—with the frequency of lunar eclipses, and run two hours or longer about once for every full moon. And even then I barely nudge the lower border of "hard." So why, you might ask, do pesky injuries—thought to be linked to hard effort—continue to occur? Several answers:

For one, I've learned too many medical terms while editing doctors' books, and this has made me something of a hypochondriac. For another, my legs still carry the legacy of too many past races and long runs. A final potential culprit is a last remnant of pace-based training. That's the faster-than-normal mile that I run frequently.

"Normal" pace on the other runs, and on warm-up for and cool-down after the timed mile, is unknown. I haven't planned, checked, or recorded it in 30 years. The effort is nearly always comfortable—whatever that might mean. It feels right on that day and at that moment, and I never need to know what the pace reads.

This all changes, though, when I run the timed mile. Let's be honest here: It hasn't been truly fast since Lyndon Johnson was in the White House. But speed is relative. Dipping far below normal pace is "fast," no matter what the clock says, and here I am running as much as two minutes faster than usual.

A mile run this way can hurt. The onetime miler in me says, "They're supposed to hurt." Then the older runner in me answers, "Yes, maybe the mile should be uncomfortable in the doing; that's honest effort. But the hurting shouldn't last days and weeks afterward; that's an injury." Something is wrong with a run that leads to injury. It either must be fixed or dropped.

The puzzle I had to solve a few years ago was this: How do I avoid the pressure of running against the watch, while still getting the gratifying payoff for this effort that a stopped time gives? The answer was surprisingly simple: Make this a combination of effort-based and pace-based running.

The mile became effort-based in that I no longer set any goal or checked any splits. I went into the run with no notion of what the final time should be. I didn't let the watch push my legs and lungs where they didn't care to go that day.

I took no splits. The mile remained pace-based only when I looked at the final time, which now came as a surprise. That time had determined itself without any interference from my head. I refused to let the watch's verdict, and how it compared with other recent miles, tell me whether to celebrate or mourn.

The final time now reflects more clearly what the legs and lungs wanted to do. The efforts that went into the time were appropriate to the day. On a normal-effort day I run what feels like 10K race pace. On a lower-effort day I ease off to about half-marathon pace. On a higher-effort day I rev up to 5K pace. I trust instinct and experience to tell me what's okay, and they seldom lie.

Jack Foster

I've always liked his comment that we pay too much attention to time, especially as age slows us down. He said, "If you don't look at the watch, the racing feels the same way it always did." This story on Foster ran in the October1995 *Running Commentary*.

Age isn't what it once was. In the slim biographical booklet that he wrote in 1974, Jack Foster referred to himself as an "ancient marathoner." He was then in his early 40s and seemed old at a time when masters were just beginning to claim special age groupings for themselves. Forty isn't old now, when masters' lives just begin at that age. But Foster never thought of himself as a young master. He was the oldest of the open runners.

The New Zealander is 63 now and long out of the racing headlines. Before updating his story, let's review what he once did. He ran a 2:11:19 marathon at age 41. The time stood for 16 years as a world masters record, and it remains the fastest on a loop course. (John Campbell, another New Zealander, ran 2:11:04 at point-to-point Boston in 1990.)

Foster competed against the best of the young for as long as he could. When, at about age 50, he couldn't keep up with them anymore, he retired. Sort of. This meant backing down on the running, but never stopping. And it meant picking up the pace of his original sport, bicycling.

He downplays his running, going so far as to say, "I feel like a fraud completing your questionnaire. But I do run *some*, so I'll answer it." Like many postcompetitive runners, Foster chooses what he likes best from his past program and discards all else. His favorite session was, and still is, a run as long as $1\frac{1}{2}$ hours over hilly farmlands. He now takes it two or three times a week, and nothing more.

Foster still races, too. He calls it "indulging in a fun run now and then, but at about half-throttle while finding someone to chat with." His "half-throttle" on half-training is a pace that few 63-year-olds can match—a 37-minute 10K, for instance. A month or two of full training and a few full-bore races could make him a record setter again. But after all he did in his 40s, he has nothing left to prove in his 60s.

TIMELESS RACING

Our earliest habits die the hardest. I come from a time-conscious tradition, modeling myself after a track-fan dad who taught me to read his stopwatch soon after I learned to tell time. Later, while racing on the track myself, I plotted and recorded splits down to the tenth-second for every half-lap. This habit didn't transfer well to the roads, and especially not to my first marathon.

I ran it at Boston, which then drew checkpoint lines at odd places such as 6.7 and 17.6 miles. Translating these splits into pace per mile and projecting a final time overtaxed my midrace computing skills. So I ran blind, holding the pace that felt right without knowing exactly what it was until the marathon ended. The final time surprised me by being 15 minutes faster than hoped.

Hopes immediately grew. I thought: If this is possible without knowing pace, think what can happen with planning. My mara-

Leslie Pawson (left) and Johnny Kelley in the 1938 Boston Marathon.

thon splits were never this unplanned again. I'd write them on my race number or on tape stuck to the wristband of my watch. They would never let me go as fast as I had while trusting instinct to set the pace at Boston.

Splits seldom come up exactly as planned, meaning they're less likely to improve a race than to disrupt it. "Too slow" a split causes an unwise acceleration beyond that day's ability. "Too fast" a split causes an unnatural holding back.

Mark Nenow ran the fastest 10K pace in U.S. track history, as well as on the roads. Yet he never thought much about his pacing. Nenow's plan was simply "to stick my nose in it and run with the leaders as long as I can. That way I either make a breakthrough or die like a dog." He once set his 5000m PR on the way to a 10,000m. If he'd known it was this fast, he might have thought death was imminent and backed way off the pace. Instead he held it, breaking through with almost a minute's improvement of his 10K time.

This timeless approach to pacing impressed me when I heard Mark speak of it in 1984, the year he set a U.S. 10K road best that still stands. But I wasn't yet ready to leave my watch at the starting line, or to wear earplugs and blinders to keep from hearing or seeing any split times. The old habit of checking progress reports dies hard.

Later, though, a race gave me no choice about running timeless. This half-marathon neglected to mark any of its miles or to post any clocks along the way. I joined the complainers that day as we ran along not knowing the score. Without the usual time reminders, I had to fall back on instinct and into the pace that felt right. This race turned out to be my best at any distance in the 1990s. As in that long-ago Boston Marathon, the internal clock worked better than the one on my wrist.

TIME OUT

Jumbo Elliott, whose coaching reputation matched his first name, taught his Villanova runners to manage their time well. "Live by the clock," he told them. Elliott was never my coach. I never even met the guy. But at an impressionable age I took his admonition to heart, and then to extremes.

Thirty-some years later I still live by the clock. My wake-up time—no alarm clock needed—is the same every day, and so are bedtime, writing, and eating times. Not just approximately the same, but exactly. Running, leaning as heavily as it does on precious minutes and seconds, created this compulsion and now feeds it.

Ask me any race time I've ever run, and I'll tell you within a second—meaning both the time it takes to come up with that result and the accuracy of the time itself. I go so far as to record my daily runs by time periods, not distances. These runs, of course, always end at precisely the scheduled time—usually 60 or 30 minutes and not a minute more or less.

This sense of timing didn't pass to my youngest child, daughter Leslie. Though she has Down's syndrome, she can read the numbers on a clock but places little value on them. She splits time no finer than "then" and "now," "soon" and "later." When we're together, we operate more by her sense of time than mine. This gives me a needed time-out from my compulsion.

Good example: One Sunday we took a run together. Well, I ran and she rode along on her bicycle. This was progress. Leslie has had a prolonged childhood, and I've missed many runs because she couldn't stay home alone. Even when I went out without her, the time away was unsettling. I worried that an inattentive sitter would let her wander off, and I'd sometimes hide Leslie's shoes to limit her range.

When she learned to ride a bike and I rode mine, we could range widely together. But this was our first bike-run attempt. Dad planned to run an hour—no more or less. Daughter had no such plans. I wanted to fill the time with running. She wanted to fill the time, and then some, with whatever she felt like doing at any moment.

Leslie stopped to take off her extra clothes as the morning warmed. She stopped to argue at a fork in the path about the direction she wanted to take and I didn't. She stopped to talk with friendly dogs and to chuck rocks into the water. She finally stopped riding and chose to run-walk the final half-mile to the car, leaving me to push her bike.

I have no idea how long this session was, or how many of these minutes were run. Only a wild guess went into my diary. For once, time didn't count this day. Only the father-daughter experience did, and it meant no less for not knowing exactly how long it had lasted.

5

Listening to the Heart

We must all follow our hearts, literally or figuratively,

when selecting the proper training effort. Some

runners might decide to listen to every note by way

of a heart rate monitor, while others choose to hear

only the overall tune that the body plays.

CHECKING YOUR PULSE

Thanks, John Gallagher, for finally convincing me to listen more closely to my heart. I'd heard this advice before—from friends Sally Edwards and John Parker, Roy Benson and Ellen Sampson—but never heeded it until now.

John Gallagher is a man of many talents and multiple businesses. He's a coach, massage therapist, and running-store owner from his base in Salem, Oregon. Since 1988 he has used, coached with, and proclaimed the benefits of *effort-based training*. John was my final convincer, by way of an article he wrote for *Marathon & Beyond* magazine (and from which I promise to steal none of his lines). From him I bought my first heart rate monitor (HRM).

This purchase is as shocking a confession for me to write as it is for you to read. Normally I'm Low-Tech Joe, who has in past stories railed against runner sunglasses, "new-and-improved" shoes, and all socks. My shoes are closeouts and blemished seconds. My

© Ken Lee

watch, the longtime monitoring device of choice, sells for less than a year's worth of newsletters.

So what possessed me to buy an HRM costing more than all the other running equipment I own combined? One answer is general, the other personal.

The monitor is not an expensive yuppie-runner toy, but a valuable tool. Experts from George Sheehan on down have long advised us, "Listen to the body." The monitor gets specific on where to listen and what exactly to listen for there.

All runners already monitor their work some way, and mostly by the least-accurate method. Their training and racing are pace-based. They time all their miles, then let the per-mile average dictate how to react to the day's run. They struggle to hold a constant, preordained pace when the heart and lungs and legs would prefer a slower one that day—or they hold back artificially when the body feels frisky.

Heart-rate training is effort-based. You run at a constant effort—which varies from day to day, even minute to minute—and don't worry about the pace. These praises I sing to effort-based training, and by extension to heart monitoring, aren't so shocking when you know my history. I've centered my running on efforts instead of paces since the 1960s.

The runs I started taking back then were all about effort—as in easing it down from everything-fast, everything-measured, every-thing-timed running that was killing my legs along with my enthusiasm. I soon stumbled onto a trick that kept the running effort-based. This was to quit measuring and counting miles, and run instead by time periods (see chapter 4).

Time-running automatically adjusts the effort. An hour run can't be made to end any sooner than 60 minutes, so the natural tendency here is to find the right pace for the day and groove into it. How do I define and measure *right*?

YOUR OWN BEST BEAT

If you need exact numbers for what effort is right, you're asking the wrong guy. Ask John Gallagher instead. The best I can say is: If it feels right, then it usually is right.

Think of dialing the proper effort in terms of riding a multispeed bicycle. I suppose the pros have tables telling them how many

RPMs to maintain, and when exactly to shift into higher or lower gears. But casual riders don't need anything that fancy. They just shift into the gear that feels right at the moment—lower for uphills, higher for down. Speeds change, but the gears even out the effort.

The "gearing" of the human body is much more sophisticated. A bike might have 3, 10, or 18 gears, but the body has hundreds. Yet our shifting remains simple. We shift into the gear that feels right. This can be very low and slow to very high and fast, with dozens of degrees of difference in between.

I'd long done this shifting automatically. Then John Gallagher asked me to preview his article on heart rate monitors before he shipped it to *Marathon & Beyond*, and convinced me to try one. The early tests were comical. I don't call myself Low-Tech Joe just because I'm simple or cheap. I'm also a mechanical klutz.

The first time I strapped the HRM's band across my rib cage, the monitoring watch flat-lined. Oops! I'd put on the sensor upside down. When the watch finally pounded out a steady resting beat, I took it to the streets. My pulse shot above 200 in the first block.

Considering my projected maximum was about 180, something was seriously amiss here. Potentially fatal arrhythmia in progress? If so, I was in the right place—passing a fire station that housed a team of paramedics who could quiet the runaway rhythm. Strangely, the racing beat quieted on its own within another block. But the same 200-plus figure appeared again as I passed the fire station. If in doubt, check the directions. The guidebook warned that radio transmitters, such as those that alerted the medics, might interfere with the HRM signal. Mystery solved.

The real pulse rates posed no mystery. I played a little game, trying to guess what the reading would be before looking at my wrist. Even being new to the device, I could come within a couple of beats. This takes no special talent. Anyone with experience at running by effort knows how the slightest variations feel, and the HRM simply adds numbers to those old familiar feelings.

Wearing the monitor for a week or so convinced me that I didn't need to know the exact numbers. They added an unwanted layer of complexity to my running. Sorry, John Gallagher and all the other promoters of this product, but I no longer use it. Yet, I don't want to leave anyone thinking I'm discounting its potential value to certain people. It can be the salvation of many troubled runners:

- Those who run too hard on their "easy" days and need permission to slow down.

John Gallagher

When the material in this chapter on heart rate monitors origi-nally appeared in *Running Commentary*, I gave Gallagher a chance to respond. He uses the monitor for his coaching in Salem, Oregon. Here is Gallagher's reply.

The only place we might differ is I'd be a bit more careful with the underlying assumption of runners "knowing their bodies." If your readers are primarily old track and road-racing dogs with years of experience (and injuries to prove it), then "going by effort" is great. They have probably learned effort-based training the hard way—through years of trial and error. However, if many of your readers are in the novice category with 2 to 4 years of running experience, I can't emphasize enough how valuable the HRM can be in deciphering the language of the body so they *can* read it.

The old dogs are going to stick with running. I'm not so sure about the young pups (regardless of age). When those novices start getting to their PR plateau, and the aches and pains start showing up, they might move on to another activity. The HRM can give those novices a measuring stick the old dogs have operated on for years. It can also help them avoid falling into the traps of overtraining and overracing.

No matter how many articles you or I or anyone else writes trying to explain pacing, you have to *feel* it against a measuring stick of some sort. Pacing is not a purely intellectual concept. For today's novices, the HRM can teach the language of the body by providing numbers and alarms similar to the coaches and their whistles that monitored and guided our efforts years ago.

Also, I'd like to add the following to your litany of salvation for troubled runners:

- Those who run too hard on their "easy" days and need permission to slow down. Recovery runs should be between 60 and 70 percent of max effort—truly an easy jog.

- Those who have not mastered the powerful training tool of tempo runs. An HRM can keep you fine tuned at the required 85 to 87 percent effort, building your aerobic strength without turning your workout into a race.

- Those who get a little too competitive (whether consciously or unconsciously) during their training runs. The HRM will keep you from racing your training buddies during practice.

- Those who run too easily on their "hard" days and need an outside force to apply the whip.

- Those who go too fast early in races, or slow down too much later, and need to smooth out their efforts.

- Those who need to equalize the variables of weather, terrain, and mismeasured courses that play havoc with pace.

- Those who are more bothered than I am with the slowdown of age and need assurance that their efforts remain constant.

We must all follow our hearts, literally or figuratively. Some runners (like those named above) may decide to listen to every note, while others (like me) may choose to hear only the overall tune.

EXTRA EFFORTS

Blood pressure. Any mention of those two words seized my attention after my BP started testing borderline high. It's a family trait from which my chronic running habit hasn't excused me. So when Paul Williams spoke of his research in *Runner's World*, my eyes landed on blood pressure as if he'd highlighted the words in red type. My first reaction to abnormal readings had been to ease the running even more than usual. I cut total mileage, and dropped all racing and faster training miles.

Wrong choice, says Williams. The PhD epidemiologist conducted the National Runner's Health Study that looked into the habits and health of 10,000 men and women who run. The data led him to the conclusion that more is better—more mileage, more effort—if a runner wants to promote heart health. "Our earlier data showed that as your weekly mileage goes up, your cholesterol profile improves," Dr. Williams told Adam Bean of *RW*. Even after the cuts, my mileage wasn't bad, and my blood-fat profiles tested boringly normal.

But just putting in the miles isn't enough, said Williams. "Interestingly, our just-published research shows that mileage isn't the whole story. Training intensity also seems to play a key role." He explained, "Basically as training intensity increases, so do the benefits to your heart . . . . Intense training—speedwork, racing, hills—seems to do more for lowering blood pressure."

Those two words! Now he had my full attention. My BP hadn't eased with the lowering of efforts.

Dr. Williams parts company with the advocates of easy exercise. He said, "What I don't like is the implication that this [low-mileage, low-effort activity] is the optimum, and that more exercise isn't necessary or [is] even harmful. It is my belief that training intensity is probably more important than mileage when it comes to fending off heart disease."

In other words, to get personal here, the easy runs and walks that made up most of my week's efforts after my BP scare might have become too effortless. Maybe I wasn't pushing hard enough to keep my bloodlines in shape. How to make the efforts better? Simply running more days was a worthwhile start because any running, even the easiest type, was more work than doing nothing.

Running more days worked for Tom Mann, a longtime reader of my newsletter and a longer-time runner. The last time I saw Tom, he stood beside the road at the Big Sur Marathon, looking ghost-like. He'd intended to run that race but had passed out while riding the bus to the start. A rhythm disturbance in his heart was to blame.

I heard from him a year later. He didn't mention his heart but wrote, "My running has gone through a wonderful six months or so of really feeling like a runner again. I shed about 10 ugly pounds and started doing a little speedwork. Within two weeks I was like a new person. I even started running races again."

Like me, Tom had thought the way to treat his shaky cardiovascular system was to run shorter and slower. In fact, we needed just the opposite. I restored a little of the lost effort—adding back a fast mile or two a week, and returning to the races. My blood pressure dropped from borderline-scary to high-normal. Even if it hadn't budged, though, the upping of effort would have been worthwhile because it made me feel more like a runner again.

THREE-PART HARMONY

What you did before you knew what you were doing can be instructive. Sometimes it also can be right. Untutored instincts guided me into the mile as my first race 40 years ago, and I've raced that distance hundreds of times. While no longer competing on the track, a timed mile is still my preferred fast run. When my running shifted into a longer and slower gear more than 30 years ago, most

© Richard Etchberger

runs weren't all that long. My favorite length then was one hour, and this is where the long running still begins.

But in recent years another old friend, the easy half-hour run, fell out of the inner circle. Dropping these easy runs in favor of rest days cut me off from one-third of my running roots. Some of my earliest runs traced the checkerboard squares of Iowa farmland—one mile to a side, four miles in all, about 30 minutes in time. These easy runs—combined with a few longer ones and a few shorter, faster ones—led to my healthiest running and best racing.

Early on I'd struck this balance of long-fast-easy without knowing what I was doing. It took me a long time and a lot of erring in one direction or the other to see what had been right from the start. In the early 1960s I tipped out of balance on the fast side without enough long running. In the late 1960s and early 1970s my average run grew long, but I didn't go fast enough. Then through the 1980s the routine gradually evolved to all easy, nothing long or fast. I never missed a day, but much was missing.

I wanted more from running than no-stress half-hours. I wanted to stretch out the distance or to stretch out my stride. To go longer and faster, while retaining a sense of balance, I started taking my first voluntary rest days. Long and fast eventually became my whole program. I'd run an hour one day, a timed mile the next, and rest the third.

Sometimes I'd run longer than an hour or race. Then I'd take even more rest days afterward. I went so far as to write: "There is no such thing as an easy run. The quickest and surest way to recover is to rest." I'd given up half-hour runs in favor of rests, and this was no way to treat an old friend.

Finally I brought the three pieces of my history together by restoring the easy runs and resting less. I'd been taking as many as three days a week off. Now I've replaced two of those rests with easy runs (while retaining one free day so I'll never get caught up in streaking mania again). The extra runs require little effort, but they do this runner's heart a lot more good—in the figurative if not the literal sense—than doing nothing.

6

Finding Shoes That Fit

It's as much an oversimplification to say that shoes cause injuries as to claim that they prevent injuries. In both cases the shoes are probably minor players. The main cause of injuries has always been, probably still is, and may always be mistakes in the way we run. Meaning: too much, too fast, too often.

SHOE SAFETY

A story out of Canada got lots of ink and airplay on both sides of the border. I first heard it on National Public Radio, then received a Toronto *Globe & Mail* story from Canadian friend John McGee. The newspaper article's provocative headline: "Pricey Shoes Over-rated, Report Says." Its subhead read, "Cheap footwear offers just as much protection to runners as the expensive kind."

Reporter Beverley Smith's story began, "People are being duped by claims that expensive athletic footwear is safer than cheap shoes, according to a Canadian report published in the *British Journal of Sports Medicine*. Advertising claims of superior cushioning and protection create a false sense of security in the user and actually increase the chance of injury." These were the findings in a study by Steven Robbins and Edward Waked of McGill University in Montreal.

John McGee, running columnist for an Edmonton newspaper, wanted my views on the subject. The response: It's as much an oversimplification to say that shoes cause injuries as to claim that they prevent injuries. In both cases the shoes are probably minor players. The research I've read indicates that the main cause of injuries has always been, probably still is, and may always be mistakes in the way we run. Meaning: Too much, too fast, too often.

That said, I can tell you that the percentage of runners getting hurt has dropped steadily since the 1970s. Back then *Runner's World* surveys indicated that about two-thirds of runners were injured (an injury being defined as anything serious enough to disrupt the routine). The figure has since dropped to about 50 percent, which is still too high. We could take two different readings on our improving health:

1. Runners have grown smarter, or at least more conservative, in their training over the years.
2. Shoes have gotten better in their protective qualities in this time.

The answer is probably some of both, but my guess is the first factor is the more important of the two.

I've known about Steven Robbins (the main author of this study) for at least 10 years. His longstanding thesis is that the best shoe is

Jeff Johnson

The shoe story of the last third of the century has been Nike. I knew Johnson, one of that company's founders, for almost a decade before there was a company by that name. He was featured in the May 1997 *Running Commentary.*

They met as students at Stanford University in the 1960s. Both sold Tiger running shoes, first from their car trunks and later from small offices. I bought my first Tigers from one of them, Jeff Johnson, and met the other, then known by his nickname of Buck, a few years later when he came to the *Runner's World* office to introduce his new brand of shoes. He had dropped the old nickname (but lived up to it by making big bucks) and is now known as Phil Knight.

Legend has it that Jeff is responsible for naming the company. The word reportedly came to him in a dream: *Nike.* The business thrived, of course. Knight is now the most powerful business leader in sports, and Jeff Johnson is long departed from Nike. Jeff took very early retirement in 1983, when in his early 40s. He didn't have to wonder what he'd do with the rest of his life. He would do more of what he already did for fun: shoot photos for magazines, fish at his lakeside home in New Hampshire, and coach runners.

"I entered coaching in 1969, by accident actually," he recalls. "I was coerced into taking over a Boston women's club, the Liberty AC. I couldn't say no to a bunch of talented, dedicated young women." Jeff later coached at two high schools in New Hampshire. Former athletes of his occasionally call to tell him the good directions their lives have taken and how they credit track and cross-country with giving them the tools for success. "More than once I had graduating seniors tell me that they learned more in cross-country than they learned in school. Not true literally, of course, but what they meant was that they learned things in running that school didn't teach them."

Jeff has now taken a leap to coaching out-of-college athletes. This has led him back to where he started as an athlete, to the Stanford area, where he founded The Farm Team. Meanwhile his old classmate, Phil Knight, oversees an empire. Who's to say which of them is better off?

the least shoe, and that we might be best off running barefoot. I too happen to prefer the least of all shoes (see next section). While Robbins uses science to support his contention, mine is a personal preference and not a claim that anything is wrong with the way most of today's shoes are made or marketed.

My unscientific bias is that choosing shoes isn't so much a matter of safety (or even performance) as one of comfort. I'm most comfortable in light, flimsy shoes. This is out of step with most of today's runners, who feel best in more substantial models. To each their own. I don't think they're suffering for their choice, and neither am I.

LEAST OF ALL SHOES

So many shoes. So few I would use. Makers of running shoes would have us believe that the quality and selection of shoes have never been better. I'm not convinced. By my admittedly unorthodox tastes, the choices are slim and growing slimmer.

This I noticed while shopping for new shoes. The old ones were timeworn. None of the four pairs was less than a year old, not because I couldn't afford to replace them but because suitable replacements were so hard to find. This latest quest was discouraging. I visited three different stores in town and probably looked at 50 different models. Not one pair would have felt right to me.

Gone were all the models I'd worn for many years. These were soft-soled, flexible, fairly light, and reasonably cheap shoes that most of today's runners wouldn't give a second look. You wouldn't see them written about in magazine shoe issues and couldn't find them in true running stores. My choice in shoes has been decreed unsuitable for today's runners, who think they need combat boots. These are the thick-soled, inflexible, bulky, and pricey shoes that have pushed out of the stores everything I find tolerable.

So, what to do? I could go to racing shoes, but local stores carry very few of these and at higher prices ounce for ounce than the training models.

I prefer to support my friendly neighborhood running merchant instead of a faceless mail-order house. But the slim selection locally now leaves me no choice but to call an 800 number. Several companies send me their catalogs, and some advertise the "outdated" and "underweight" models that work best for me. The trouble with ordering by mail is that I can't give the shoes a lift-bend-and-squeeze test. I don't know how they feel and fit until I've committed the cash, but it's a gamble worth taking.

One option no longer available to me is going shoeless. My running passed through a barefoot phase in the early 1960s. I won cross-country races this way in high school and ran my best time on Drake University's three-mile course with nothing coming between me and the grass.

I'm stuck with shoes now. But I can read with nostalgic longing the story of Charlie Robbins. His old friend, *Runner's World* editor Amby Burfoot, interviewed him for the online *RW*. Amby introduced "Doc" Robbins as a national champion at the marathon and several other distances in the 1940s. Now in his 70s, he continues a longtime habit of running barefoot or nearly so.

When he talked with Amby at a Connecticut race, Robbins wore a pair of knee socks covered with aqua-socks. This was overdressing by his usual standards. "Why did you stop wearing shoes?" Amby asked. Robbins said, "I first got the idea when I was 15 and running cross-country in high school. I thought it was more natural and good for your running form. Later I began thinking that we've had 5 million years of evolution and never developed a raised heel, so we probably weren't intended to run on heels. I land almost flat-footed, and I've had very few injuries."

I'm no Charlie Robbins. I've developed a dependence on raised heels, as well as orthotics inside my shoes. Also, I don't land flat-footed, but I am a prancer. So maybe I'll never again run a barefoot step. But I can and will continue to seek out the least shoes available and tolerable.

BIGFOOT SIGHTINGS

You've heard the phrase "long of tooth." It suggests that teeth keep growing as we get older. Noses seem to grow more prominent too, with age. Hair may grow faster on men's ears and women's chins.

I'd heard all this. But I didn't suspect that another effect of aging could be bigger feet. Oh, sure, I knew that foot growth was a temporary result of running. That's why we're told to try on shoes after a run or late in the day, to allow for the half-size of swelling that normally occurs in hard-working feet.

Paul Reese experienced this effect to the extreme while running across the United States at age 73. He reports in *Ten Million Steps*, a book about his 3200-mile run, that after the first few million steps his shoes became too snug. "By the end of yesterday's run," he wrote in his diary from somewhere in Kansas, "I found my feet have swollen so much that my shoes are now a half-size too small. They are beginning to cause pain and could lead to blisters."

Reese hadn't thought to bring along larger shoes and couldn't immediately find any replacements. "My only course of action," he said then, "is to cut out the toebox in my present ones and see what happens." What happened was that he had to locate bigger and bigger shoes as the distance added up. His feet eventually swelled a total of $1\frac{1}{2}$ sizes, or half a size for each 1000 miles. They returned to normal size about a week after the trek ended.

Foot growth doesn't always come and go as it did with Reese. It can also sneak up on a runner and become permanent. As part of my compulsion for record keeping, I've long made note of shoe changes: which brand, model and, yes, size. The records show that my feet are bigger now than ever before.

I started running as a teenager in size 8 shoes. At about my 30th birthday, long after I'd stopped growing, the size went to $8\frac{1}{2}$. The shoes fit the same way for almost 20 years. No matter which company made the shoe, I could count on $8\frac{1}{2}$s feeling just right.

They no longer do. The forefoot feels too tight, and the heels pinch. I've now jumped to a size 9. Shoe sizing hasn't changed; my feet have. Running and age have added a full size in my middle years.

While working with Joe Ellis, DPM, on his book *Running Injury-Free*, I found a possible explanation. Dr. Ellis described the *Bigfoot Syndrome* that he sees in some middle-aged patients: "Several times a year, one will come into the office and tell me that his feet are still growing. He'll say, 'It's the weirdest thing, Doc. I have been a size $10\frac{1}{2}$ most of my life, and over the last few years I have grown a full shoe size.'"

Falling arches are to blame, said Ellis. "The change in size is a giveaway. As the arch falls, the foot gets longer. There isn't any true growth, but the flattening of the arch has lengthened the foot." He added that "arches don't collapse overnight. They almost always fall gradually."

The first symptom you'll notice will be in shoe comfort. A size that once felt just right will now feel too tight. Take pride in the bigger feet. You've earned them by putting the necessary time and miles on them.

TESTING TECHNOLOGY

Bill Rodgers, already our sport's record holder for frequent-flyer miles, is making more than his usual rounds lately. This time I saw him in Victoria, British Columbia, where he'd flown from his East Coast home to promote his book, *Bill Rodgers' Lifetime Running Plan.*

About that same time an interview with Bill appeared in *U.S. News and World Report.* One of Marc Silver's questions: "Do you like gadgets?" Bill acknowledged that "technology has brought us better shoes and better running gear." He named another current example: "Heart rate watches are a good training device."

Bill Rodgers.

That said, Bill told a story that to him illustrated runaway technology: "I recently saw a runner wearing a big backpack with a tube coming out in front. He looked like an alien from *Star Wars*. Then I realized he was going to do a long run and was carrying water with him." That's not something Bill would do. "I'm not real high tech in terms of running," he told the interviewer. "The more you keep running simple, the more you will stay with it."

I think along those same lines. Someone once asked me, "What do you know about creatine phosphate?" All I knew about this dietary supplement was that I had to look up its spelling.

I'm low tech in an increasingly high-tech running world. Heart rate monitors are the new measures of effort and pace. Well-equipped marathoners of my pace carry their own drinks and eats in a fanny pack. Nose Band-Aids make runners look like NFL

© Ken Lee

wannabes. We have gels to swallow and to wear in our shoes. Watches do everything but cook our breakfast. Shirts and shorts leave little of the anatomy to the imagination.

I'm slow to chase the latest fads and fashions, but not entirely a fuddy-duddy. I've just seen too many miracles-that-weren't to leap after everything new-and-improved. I prefer to wait and watch as the marketplace dictates the survival prospects of products. A 10-year test will surely separate the useful from the frivolous. Any product still selling well a decade after its introduction must work. Anything that doesn't will be gone.

The basic digital stopwatch is one prominent survivor. It remains our best measure of performance (though not necessarily of effort; see chapter 5). For every product that passes the test, 10 fail. Shoes have advanced more than any other category of product, yet the shoe companies have made plenty of missteps.

Remember the LD-1000 with its widely splayed tailfins, or the Varus Wedge that tilted to the outside? Inflatable shoes and shoes with springs instead of sponge have come and gone.

We've had Hanteens for combining water carrying with weight work. We've had DMSO for treating soreness, the Bone-Fone for listening to music through the torso instead of the ears, the Altitude Simulator that truly looked like a prop from *Star Wars*. All are gone. Their promoters overestimated the gullibility of runners, who won't be fooled for long.

What will be the sales of heart rate monitors 10 years from now? What will become of nose Band-Aids or water backpacks? That's for us to decide.

Dealing With Downtime

Lively legs thrive on almost any type of running—long

or short, fast or slow, steady or broken with walks,

in whatever mixture feels right at the moment.

Dead legs kill the best-laid plans—and the spirit

along with them.

PAINFUL EXPERIENCE

One of my worst fears nearly came true. I won't say when or where this happened, to keep from shaming myself to the people who were there. Let's just say it could have been Anyrace, USA, in almost any year.

I fear limping to the stage, there to tell a crowd of runners how they might run better when I've clearly failed at it myself. I can hear them thinking, "Why should we listen to him when he can't even keep healthy?" Good question. I almost had to answer it recently.

Earlier that same day in Anyrace, I'd transformed a small problem in a calf muscle into a big one by running farther than my legs cared to go. Now the stiffness had set in, leaving me unable to walk normally when I climbed out of the car at the hotel where runners were gathering for the talk. I would have pulled into a handicapped parking space if I'd had the right sticker.

After hobbling a few steps from the car, I returned to fold a piece of cardboard into a makeshift heel lift. This let my injury escape detection. If the listeners had caught me limping, I would have confessed my mistakes—then quickly shifted the discussion from me to them. I would've asked, "Who here has not been hurt?" Define hurting as anything serious enough to disrupt normal running for at least a week, and few if any hands would have gone up.

As I mentioned in chapter 6, I helped Joe Ellis, DPM, write *Running Injury-Free*. That's an impossible dream, because the only runners who never get hurt are those who've never tried hard enough. *Injury-Freer* would be a more realistic title.

I'm a subscriber to the constant-pain-level theory. It says that we always run with a certain quota of pain. Most of the time this pain is scattered through various parts of the body and isn't disruptive. It only becomes a problem when it all comes together in one spot as an injury.

As one who has worked through and waited out nearly every injury known to sports medicine, I can say this about our injuries: They aren't so bad. Not bad in the pain sense, because they seldom interfere with anything in life except the runs. Not bad in the time sense, because they rarely last more than a few weeks. And not all bad in the educational sense, because pain is a great teacher.

There's nothing like an injury to make a runner study what went wrong, and finally to fix it. This calf problem showed me that I'd

Priscilla Welch

In the space of little more than 10 years, Welch went from non-runner, to the best in the world for her age, to cancer survivor. Her story appeared in the March 1996 *Running Commentary.*

Priscilla Welch started late in running. She was almost 35 then, and had already lived enough to acquire perspective. She often said, while standing at the peak of her running career, that this was a "pleasant interlude." It occupied a space between life as she'd known it and whatever was to follow after her running eased down.

MARS LONDON MARATHON '87
SEIKO TIMING
2.26.51
TANDEM COMPUTERS
Mars

© Photo Run/Victah Sailer

The interlude included coming within three places of an Olympic medal when nearly 40. At 42, she set the world masters marathon record of 2:26:51 that no woman has approached in more than eight years. At almost 43 she beat all women in the New York City Marathon. Priscilla intended to become the first woman over 50 to run a marathon under 2:40 but didn't get the chance.

About three years ago Priscilla was diagnosed with breast cancer. Treatment took a long time, and took a lot out of her. We worked together on the book *Masters Running and Racing* in 1990, but had fallen out of touch after that. Then we reconnected last summer when I interviewed her for another book. Priscilla, now 51, downplays her struggle and writes in the same upbeat, anything's-possible style that filled her earlier, precancer book. "I'm getting it together better," says her handwritten note at the end of the form letter. "The body is ready to go again after a very long time recovering from the effects of chemo."

Chemotherapy treatments ended in mid-1993, but she still requires checkups twice a year. They've all found her to be disease-free. "I feel the body could do almost anything it wanted to now, providing the mind wants it too," she writes. "I'm still training and running, but have quite a ways to go before I can get back to where I was. It is possible; we know that. But it is quite a confusing time for me still—indecision, lack of total commitment, and the loss of full concentration in anything." She views this as "yet another transition time which will blossom into something good real soon." (Two years after this story ran, Priscilla Welch remained cancer-free—and her world masters marathon record remained unbeaten.)

run a little harder and rested less often the past couple of months, then ignored the early warnings of trouble that predictably appeared. Now the legs had my full attention, and I vowed to listen more closely to what they were telling me.

There's also nothing like an injury to remind us of what's really important in running. I thought my big goal was to run a marathon that spring. Now it was just to run, period. And I would. All the painful experiences of the past assured me that this one too would pass, but not before leaving behind reminders of what works best and what counts most.

HAPPY LEGS

Happy legs is how Jeff Galloway described the ideal condition of a runner. Speaking at one of his running camps, he said, "Check in with your legs and decide how happy they are before deciding exactly what to do that day."

Jeff Galloway traveled next to Canada, and left an impression there with Terry Carlyle. The orthodontist wrote of finishing, undertrained, the Edmonton Marathon in $4\frac{1}{2}$ hours by a Galloway-inspired plan of run five minutes, walk one. "My ego was not happy," wrote Carlyle, "but my legs were."

I first met Anne Audain at a Galloway event in Atlanta 15 years ago. Jeff never coached her, and she doesn't talk of her legs being "happy." But they surely are. Audain, a three-time New Zealand Olympian, has never been injured. "I've learned to read my body very well," she told *Runner's World* writer Bob Cooper.

A well-read body's legs stay happy. When I read my schedule more closely than my body, the result usually is unhappy legs. Happy is more than healthy, which is merely the absence of injury. Happy means lively, full of bounce and energy.

My legs return to happiness very slowly after marathons. By trying to rush the recovery after one mid-1990s attempt at this distance, I ended up extending the comeback period from the usual few weeks to several months. Finally over that dead-legged period, I tried to make up for the lull in racing by overracing—65 kilometers of it in four events over a six-week period. This resulted in injuries in one calf and then the other.

Finally over those problems, I saw with 20/20 hindsight what had gone wrong. My main problem, as it is for most runners whose legs become chronically unhappy, is that I forgot what not to run:

- Not taking at least one easy day per kilometer of the last race before running another race.

- Not heeding the warnings of my legs to stop for the day after as little as one mile when they don't feel right.

- Not stopping to rest often enough, which for me means one day a week, minimum.

These three nonrun rules are the keys to keeping my legs happy, which is the key to everything. Lively legs thrive on almost any type of running—long or short, fast or slow, steady or broken with walks, in whatever mixture feels right at the moment. Dead legs kill the best-laid plans—and the spirit along with them.

SLEEPING SICKNESS

A great talent of mine is one I practice nightly but privately. I'm a champion sleeper. I can sleep eight full hours any night, no matter what worries race through my head at bedtime. This skill annoys my wife, a fretful sleeper. It used to concern my parents, who wondered why I didn't sleep the normal postmidnight to midday hours of a teenager. Now my habit amuses a friend named Chuck Palmer. He never tries to contact me after what he calls my "narcolepsy hour," which comes early.

The flip side of this sleep skill is that I need all these hours. I'm slow-footed and slow-witted if I fall even one hour short of my usual eight. Two or more hours under the quota, and I risk bigger disruptions.

Here I'll slip in a statement from Dick Brown. He's a PhD exercise scientist as well as a coach of Olympians in three different sports. One research project dealt with "recovery indicators . . . to see if the onset of illness [or] injury could be predicted. We figured that if we could predict [an impending breakdown], we might be able to prevent it."

© Photo Run/Victah Sailer

Dick looked into 30 factors suspected of revealing excess stress. He matched them against breakdowns suffered by the runners at Nike's old club, Athletics West. Four of these factors showed the strongest correlation with illness or injury, and two of them dealt with sleep. (The others were morning heart rate and morning body weight.)

Time to bed and hours slept both counted heavily in Dick's study. He listed these warning signs: (1) getting to bed 40 or more minutes later than normal, and (2) sleeping 10-plus percent less than normal. These are small margins of error. If I usually fall asleep at 10 o'clock, staying up only until 11 could run me into trouble. If I normally sleep eight hours, dropping a single hour puts me a risky percentage below the quota. My penalty for sleep loss usually is a cold. If I'm sleeping right, I don't catch colds. If not, well . . ..

Sleep didn't come until midnight before this midsummer trip. Then I woke up at four o'clock to catch the early flight. No problem, I thought. I'll make up for that loss with a nap. I'm also a champion napper.

As soon as I laid down for that nap, a tap sounded at the door. "Steve, are you in there?" asked a juvenile voice. That night I dropped into bed early, and quickly fell unconscious. Later the ring of the phone jolted me awake. "Is Steve there?" asked a voice as young as the one I'd heard earlier. "No," I growled at the girl before slamming down the receiver. Sleep was slow to return.

I could absorb one short night, but not two in a row. The next morning I woke up with an ominous tickle in my nose and throat. These symptoms soon blew up into a nasty cold that cost me five days of running. This cold wasn't the result of exposure to germs, or to chills, or to overwork. It came from not taking the preventive medicine of sleep in proper dosage.

FINISH LINES

We'll just call him Jim here and say that he's from the Midwest. Jim is one of those longtime friends I've never met. My newsletter, *Running Commentary*, had gone out to him each month for many years. Then he sent back a letter of his own. It was the best cancel-my-subscription notice I've ever received, but it came for the worst of reasons.

Nonrenewing subscribers usually just vanish at the end of their terms. They ignore the renewal card, and I never know why we lost touch. Jim told why, after first saying that the newsletter "was a big part of my running life, and I looked forward to it every month. I started running the year I turned 40. Ran my first race, a 10K, six months later and my first marathon about eight months after that. I am 57 now and was one of those people who said they would run the rest of their life. But my body no longer lets me do it."

He told of gradually losing energy and endurance over the past 10 years. Once a 2000-mile-a-year man, his totals over the past few several years had slipped to 1800, 1500, 500, 100, "and now none. I sometimes have to take a breather after walking up one flight of stairs." His doctors first suspected a heart problem, but tests showed otherwise. "They now think I have fibromyalgia, which is a lot like chronic fatigue syndrome," he said.

Jim apologized for not extending his *Running Commentary* subscription. Then he explained, "Each month I receive it, it is a reminder of what I can no longer do and how much I miss it." My reply was that of a sympathetic runner, not a publication promoter. I didn't try to talk him out of canceling but instead said he was living out a runner's greatest fear: that a permanent injury or illness would prevent us from going on.

"You seem to be facing such a sentence," I told him, "and I can understand your feelings about wanting to distance yourself from the sport. Heck, I feel this way even when temporarily sidelined." This is the only time when my job of dealing with runners becomes unpleasant.

I had no medical advice to give Jim. He'd probably had his fill of that the past few years. But I did urge him not to abandon all hope. While dealing with thousands of runners for all these years, I wrote, I've seen very few conditions that are permanent (other than the ultimate finish line that several past subscribers, notably Jim Fixx and George Sheehan, have reached). Keep pushing the medical buttons, and maybe you'll hit the right one.

Jim's reply: "I hope someday to contact you with a request for a renewal because I'm back out on the roads. My goal is to someday run one more marathon." For now he would settle on "recovering to the point where I can at least jog a little. When you're down to nothing, you gain new appreciation for small things."

Heeding the Early Warnings

Running doesn't make us immortal. But it does make us sensitive to what isn't right, which can lead to early detection when treatment does the most good.

GETTING TO THE HEART

When Tony Sagare walked up at the Royal Victoria Marathon and introduced himself, the name didn't register on me at first. I'd read his name many times, but to me it should have sounded Italian—*cigar* with an "ay" on the end. He pronounced it more the French way—*Sa-gair*.

I soon realized our connection and almost hugged him as if he were an old friend. For years he'd read my newsletter, and I'd read his writing in *Hard-Core Runners News*, the publication of his club based in Yakima, Washington. It was there soon after our meeting that I read later about his illness. This report told of another recent connection of ours.

His story is far more serious than mine. But we went through similar crises of confidence in our health after meeting and running at Victoria. We heard two of the worst words that a runner can hear: heart problem. This diagnosis is frightening, depressing, and embarrassing.

It first causes the imagination to run wild and seems to spell the end of life as we've known it. And it allows acquaintances who don't run to say, "See how much good all that running did you?" As if heart protection were the only reason we ran. As if we still believed that running itself granted immortality. As if family history and diet didn't have as much to do with these problems as exercise habits.

Tony Sagare embodied his club's name. He was hard core to the extent of celebrating his 50th birthday (eight years earlier) by running 50 miles, and he taught fitness at a YMCA. He knew enough about his body to see that it wasn't working right. "I didn't feel pressure or tightness in my chest," he said. "It was more of a funny feeling. I didn't feel I had any energy. It seemed I was working twice as hard as I should have to go up a couple of flights of stairs, and I'd have to stop and rest."

Tony didn't go into denial, attributing the symptoms to a passing illness or delayed recovery from his last marathon. He didn't try to wait out this episode. Instead he rushed to a cardiologist, whose tests revealed two near-blockages of one artery. Tony underwent a procedure called an atherectomy to clear the obstructions.

"You never want to have the mistaken idea that running will give a special status," he said later. "There is no guarantee." Tony

© Photo Run/Victah Sailer

wrote his own guarantee for a better future by doing what had to be done, and quickly. He said of the treatment, "This is a Christmas gift to myself." The cardiologist didn't take away life as he'd known it, but opened Tony's heart to new and better ways of living.

LIFE SAVINGS

If it's true that bad things sometimes happen to good people, then it follows that those good folks can often make the best of the bad situations. I've seen plenty of examples. Two friends of mine fought illness and won. Both are men in their 50s, and both are longtime long-distance runners.

Rich Ayers directs the Trinity Hospital Hill Run in Kansas City, one of the country's best half-marathons. A mutual friend of ours took me aside at a race and asked, "Did you hear about Rich?" I'd heard nothing. "He had surgery for prostate cancer."

I sent a quick get-well message, which brought Rich's report on all he had been through. "My blood test [which screens for prostate trouble] was normal," he wrote, "but the physician found a hard spot during his digital rectal exam (DRE). So the DRE was the key in my case with no other symptoms. An ultrasound with a biopsy was ordered, and a couple of days later the physician said the biopsy samples were malignant. The next step was to decide what to do in my case, and that proved to be surgery."

He had the operation and learned that the cancer hadn't spread. However, he suffered serious complications that lingered for nearly a year. "Yes, I have had some dark days," he said later. "Life will never be the same but can still be enjoyable as I continue toward a more normal lifestyle."

Tony Sagare, whose story opened this chapter, didn't recover as well as he'd hoped from his first medical procedure. He'd undergone an atherectomy for coronary artery blockage at Christmastime. He wrote the next spring, "I watched the Boston Marathon from Providence Hospital in Yakima. I was recovering from bypass surgery performed the previous Saturday." The atherectomy procedure is given about an 80 percent chance of success—meaning 20 percent of arteries will block up again. Tony was one of the 20-percenters. "I was well back to running in late March," he said. "But somehow I really never felt like my energy level was that good, particularly when the blood supply was supposed to be better. Then symptoms almost identical to those I experienced in November recurred."

He went back for tests. Result: "One of the two arteries was blocked again, only this time more than 95 percent." Treatment: bypass surgery. He had no choice in this, he said, and the operation had to happen the next morning. "I could have had a heart attack at any time. It was very scary." Like Rich Ayers, Tony's future looks good because he got right in to see his doctor, found out what had gone bad, and did what had to be done about it. He looked ahead to better days as a result.

Running doesn't make us immortal. But it does make us sensitive to what isn't right, which can lead to early detection when treatment does the most good.

Jim Fixx

He always deserved better than to be remembered as "that guy who died while running." I recalled his greater contributions in the November 1994 *Running Commentary*.

Jim Fixx sold more books than any other running writer. His *Complete Book of Running* didn't cause the sport to boom but surely fed the forces already at work at the time of its release in 1977. The newly arrived flocks of runners had snapped up nearly a million copies of this book by 1984. That year sales

© UPI/Corbis-Bettmann

suddenly fell, along with the author. It was as if the nature and timing of his death—from a heart attack at age 52 during a training run—had suddenly canceled all the good he'd done for the sport. It was as if he'd betrayed his cause.

He had, in fact, done our sport one last favor. He'd made us face the hard truth that running isn't a cure-all. Running can build latent strengths but also uncover inherent weaknesses. Fixx's rise from pudgy smoker to trim marathoner was as dramatic as his last fall, but he seemed destined to be remembered only for the latter.

Now, 10 years after his death, *Sports Illustrated* has righted this wrong. *SI* has tipped the balance back in favor of Fixx's strong points by naming him one of the 40 leading sports figures of the magazine's lifetime. Fixx stands alone as running's representative on *SI*'s list. And why not? He deserves to be remembered for the right reason—for influencing thousands of reader-runners who have survived him. Merrill Noden wrote in *SI*: "One thing Fixx was careful not to promise readers in *The Complete Book of Running* was a longer life . . . . In the end Fixx taught us not how to make our lives longer—only how to make them better."

One of the hardest pieces I've ever done was a report on his passing in 1984. The final words of that tribute still fit him: "If Fixx could write this final chapter of his life story, he would find a light, self-effacing way of blaming himself for what happened. That was how he wrote. He wouldn't blame the sport that made his life better, if not longer. He would advise other runners to pay more attention to the precautions he ignored, but not to let his mistakes harm running's good name."

PRESSURE'S OFF

Waves of dizziness first sent me to a doctor, who sent me to another, then another. None of them ever treated the original problem. But as doctors are prone to do, they unearthed other issues to work on.

"With dizziness," said the first doctor, "we always have to suspect a heart problem. Have you ever had an EKG?" Not for at least 10 years. "So we'd better take one today." His nurse ran the resting EKG, and the doctor came back later to interpret it. "You have very dynamic heart action, which is typical for a runner," he said. "But I also see some irregularities."

He mentioned something about an "S-T segment" and "a possible problem with the left ventricle." I asked what that meant, and he dismissed the question with, "It's quite technical." So what happens now? "At the least I recommend a treadmill stress test. This should be routine for someone your age and family history."

My dad died of a stroke at 54. I have high blood pressure in both branches of the family. "Yours is running high today," said the doctor. "I'd get that evaluated, too."

This doctor had me take regular blood-pressure readings over the next several weeks. "It's high," he confirmed. "Not as high as it appears in our office, but still higher than we'd like it to be." So what do we do about it? "More testing, and then you'll probably have to start taking a blood-pressure drug." He sent me to a second doctor, who ran 60 blood and urine tests. All fell into the normal range.

My last and most dreaded doctor was the cardiologist. He would look into my heart at work and tell if it was working as it should.

We met on December 21, the darkest day of the year. A nurse led me into the "echo room," where echo (ultrasound) and EKG machines shared space the size of a walk-in closet with a treadmill and an exam table. A doctor and two technicians squeezed into this room with me.

"Nice picture!" said the doctor as my beating heart appeared on the echo screen. I don't know whether he was complimenting me on a good heart or his assistant on her good work. Probably the latter.

Resting readings taken, I jumped on the treadmill. The doctor fired questions at me and orders to his technicians as the belt rolled faster and steeper. "Let us know if you're having any problem," said the woman operating the treadmill. "I'm having one now," I said. "I'm not used to walking this fast. Can I run?"

The doctor answered. "Go right ahead." Then he asked the operator, "What is his predicted max?" The operator gave the number. "Push it up to that," said the doctor. I couldn't spot the pulse count, but he must have seen all he needed and announced, "There's no point in going further."

He now was ready to pass judgment. "Your heart is fine," he began. "No problem whatsoever except a slight thickening of the left ventricle. This could be a result of your running or a reaction to high blood pressure." I asked his advice on the mildest way to bring down the BP without shaking up my body chemistry too much. He named a drug and handed over a sample supply.

Back with my first doctor, I wanted to know, "Will I always have to take this drug?" He said, "You will as long as your untreated blood pressure remains high." But he added a note of hope. "It's up to you. If you're willing to modify your diet and control your stress, you might lower the BP enough naturally to get off the medication."

That was my assignment for the new year. My days began to brighten as I took up this challenge.

ON THE LEVEL

Fears for my heart eased, but the dizziness that had first sent me to the doctor remained. It wasn't as if I acted falling-down drunk, just a little tipsy. My equilibrium was off by a few degrees. I looked normal and pretended to be, but wasn't quite there.

Sights, sounds, and thoughts were slightly out of focus. Running, writing, and speaking (formally or socially) were never much fun, and were sometimes nauseating. The symptoms were worst when they first struck, then they waxed and waned over the next year, but never went away completely.

The first doctor I saw said, "You can take a drug and feel groggy all the time, or you can tough it out. The vertigo will probably go away on its own." I said no to drugs but soon ran out of toughness. I saw half-dozen more medical professionals during the year of living dizzily, trying to learn what was wrong and what to do about it. They ruled out the scariest possibilities but supplied no definite diagnosis or solution.

Then I got lucky. I came home from yet another doctor visit and turned on the local TV news I'd normally not watch at that hour. A report was ending with a young woman running across the screen. The voice-over said, "Her battle with vertigo appears to be won, thanks to the exercises her doctor prescribed."

I called the TV station, asking for a copy of this full piece. "We can't do that," I was told, "but we can give you a contact number." That phone number connected me with the Center for Balance Disorders in Houston. I asked for the exercises but was told, "It would be unethical for us to recommend a treatment plan without first evaluating you."

I would have taken the next flight to Houston, but the Center there had a better idea: referral to a physician doing the same type of work in Portland, a two-hour drive from home. This doctor fit me in quickly. The first exam lasted as long as the drive from Eugene. Afterward the doctor said, "We want you to take more tests, but your symptoms strongly suggest that you have...." Then he reeled off about a dozen syllables describing an inner-ear disorder.

"Did any of that make sense?" asked his nurse when the doctor left. Not much, I said, so she translated. "He says you probably have BPPV. That's benign (which means it won't kill you), paroxysmal (you sometimes have it and sometimes not), positional (quick changes in head position cause symptoms), vertigo (or imbalance)." In most cases, I was told, this condition could be treated without drugs or surgery. Specially prescribed diet and exercises could ease if not erase the symptoms.

I went on the diet. I did the exercises. And I soon felt more level-headed than at any time in the past year. A truism of medicine seems to have worked again: Look long enough and an answer usually will appear.

9

Cutting From the Diet

Little if anything is missing from our diets. We can

profit more from reducing certain items (such as fat,

sugar, salt, caffeine, and alcohol) than from adding

magic-bullet supplements or medicines.

FUN FOODS

My childhood was long past before I gave up childish things. They aren't completely gone yet in one particular area, but most of them are far enough in my past that I've consigned them to a Hall of Fame. Athletic halls of fame require retirement for at least five years for eligibility. This is how it is with the baseball and track halls, and so too with my Junk Food Hall of Fame.

Yes, I admit it; I've always been a junkie. This started young. The greatest treat that Grandma Henderson could feed us was sugar sandwiches. This nutritional nightmare started with white bread, continued with a quarter-inch of butter (or, on special occasions, whipping cream so thick it spread like butter), and ended with a half-inch of white sugar. My dad's variation was a jelly sandwich on white bread. He used so much of the sweet stuff that we asked him, "Do you want a little more bread on your jelly?"

During college, I lived two blocks from a Dairy Queen. Heaven! A day without ice cream became like one without a sunrise. Or sunset, because most of my days ended with this treat. Weather didn't matter. A zero night was no different from a 90-degree evening. After track practice, I'd trudge to DQ for my dessert— usually a cherry or butterscotch shake.

On my first job after college, I worked nights. I'd get home about 2 A.M. and sleep until 10 or 11, then wake up to a run. This meant eating my first meal at noon. I now lived near a McDonald's, where I ate my standard "breakfast" of two double cheeseburgers, a double order of fries, and a large root beer. (Never could stand the Mac's shakes, which were poor imitations of Dairy Queen's.)

Some of my happiest running years came in the mid-1970s. On Saturdays I went long with a group. After running two hours or more, we sometimes got together for breakfast (at McDonald's, where else?). More often, I indulged my appetites alone. My preferred treats: Fritos corn chips dipped in sour cream, washed down by Dr Pepper. I could follow the week's longest run with a whole bag of the chips, an entire tub of the cream, and a liter of the DP. Sometimes I'd substitute Doritos for Fritos, salsa for sour cream, Pepsi for Dr Pepper. Same effect. I loaded up on sugar, salt and fat—the Big Three dietary no-nos.

Long-term exposure to better eaters and their writings, along with a few nutrition-related health scares and the late discovery of certain food allergies, combined to clean up my dietary act some-what. All of the above-named goodies have gone into near-retire-ment as Junk Food Hall of Famers. I still honor them for the roles they played in my extended childhood and still crave them sometimes—along with Hostess fruit turnovers, buttermilk bars, or any other breakfast pastry, cherry jam with heavily buttered white bread on it, nachos in any combination as long as meat and cheese dominate, ham and pineapple pizza, and many others.

My eating is a lot healthier now. But it isn't as much fun.

© Photo Run/Victah Sailer

SWEET AND LOW

This chapter and the next confess my past dietary sins and suggest that I'm a born-again purist. I have cut down on salt, fat, and other culprits, but still haven't approached nutritional sainthood. Sugar remains my greatest temptation, to which I too often yielded in the past (and still crave). I'd long known that the sweet stuff does me no good, but this didn't slow my indulgence.

Then I learned a new and dramatic way that it does me harm. This finally convinced me to work on the sugar habit. This lesson came during testing for my stubborn case of vertigo (see chapter 8). After seeing the doctor, I went next door to talk with his nurse. She asked, "Did he mention the word 'hydrops' to you?" I'd heard it but didn't have any idea what it meant. He could have been talking about the Oreo-like cookie named Hydrox.

"Hydrops is a swelling and fluid imbalance of the inner ear," said the nurse. An injury probably caused it. She gave me a one-page handout listing the symptoms of this condition: pressure or fullness in the ears, tinnitus (ringing in the ears), hearing loss, dizziness, and imbalance. To some degree I'd felt all of these ways. Diet hadn't caused the inner-ear condition (an injury probably did), but the nurse suggested that my eating habits might aggravate the problem.

Most of the tips listed—no alcohol or caffeine, little salt—weren't concerns of mine. A tablespoon of alcohol would set my head to spinning, so I already avoided it completely. I'm not a coffee drinker, and decaf tea tastes the same to me as regular. I watch the salt as a blood-pressure precaution.

The nurse read on down the list until she found my weakness for sugar. I'd never counted sugar grams, checked product labels for added sugar, or read anywhere what "too much" might be. But I probably had revved along at 100 or more grams of sugar per day. Surely that was way too much.

Sugar spooned onto breakfast cereal wasn't the big culprit. My daily teaspoon carried only four grams. My weakness for hard candies delivered about that same amount per piece. My main source of sugar-loading came in the form of a drink I considered semihealthful. This was the bottled, fruit-flavored iced tea that I drank almost daily. One dose contained about 50 grams of sugar—or 12 teaspoons!

"You don't need to cut out sugar," said the nurse. "Just cut down. Use it sparingly, and never a large amount at one time." She added as I left, "I've had people come in here barely able to stand up. They make no change except going on the diet and show dramatic improvements."

I went right on the diet. Sugar use didn't disappear but did drop precipitously without being missed (too much). My symptoms eased. I can't say how much the lowering of sweetness helped, because it's only one part of the treatment scheme. But I can say that being back on the level tastes sweeter than any sinful food item ever did.

SHAKING THE SALT

I once spent an evening with Kenneth Cooper, MD (see chapter 2). He'd just written a book about cholesterol, and he asked if I knew mine. "No, I've never had it checked," I told him. "But I don't think it's any problem." He then ordered with the command presence of the military officer he'd once been, "Get it checked." I obeyed instantly, at the health fair where we were speaking.

I had a problem. My cholesterol read borderline high. Soon afterward, my diet changed. Nothing radical, but its fat content dropped by 10 or 15 percent. My cholesterol reading has dropped by the same percentage, well into the comfort zone.

This story had a later replay. I hadn't tracked my blood pressure and thought there was no problem with it. But there was. My doctor asked, "Do you eat a lot of salt? It can raise your blood pressure and probably contribute to the fluid imbalance in your ears." I told him I rarely salted my food.

He handed me a brochure on low-sodium diets. "Keep track of how much you eat in a day," he said. His limit is two grams a day— less than the amount in one teaspoon of salt. I learned that I'd swallowed half that amount before leaving the breakfast table. Do you know that a dry bagel contains almost half a gram of sodium, and a cup of most cold cereals carries that much more? I didn't.

Shake the salt habit, the doctors say, and blood pressure should drop. Quit using it at the table, and use much less in cooking. Start reading labels, and stay away from any item with sodium content in the hundreds per serving. Shy away from soy sauce, which is little more than liquid salt, and chips, which are platforms for salt, and anything pickled in salt. Also making the list are barbecue and spaghetti sauces, and salsa.

The cut-the-salt edict confirms again a pet theory of mine. Little if anything is missing from our diets. We can profit more from reducing certain items than from adding magic-bullet supplements or medicines. I once dumped chocolate because it caused headaches and itchy skin. I quit milk because it clogged my breathing and created teenage skin. I cut way back on fat to reduce cholesterol, but also to eat more without gaining weight.

Now I've dropped much of the salt—but not all. The goal with sodium, as it was with fat, is reduction and not deprivation. The easy way for me to control salt intake is to follow my fat practice. Set a daily limit and fill it any way I please—with one salt-bomb or spread out in small doses across the day.

With fat I set a 50-gram limit (about 25 percent of daily calories). I sometimes blow that total in one meal. But when I'm a good boy, I eat no more than a tenth of that total—or five grams—in any single item. Say the salt limit is two grams. I could go out to a Mexican or Italian dinner and get this all in one dish. Or I could eat no item that carries more than 200 milligrams of sodium. Dusting lightly all day is probably healthier than dropping one bomb.

DOWN BUT NOT OUT

You might recognize the pattern. Many runners follow it as I did during my health scares. If a little of something—from running mileage to food supplements—is good, we think that twice as much must be twice as good. If too much of something—from speedwork to dietary fat—is bad, then taking none of it must be healthiest of all.

Reacting to a blood-pressure rise, and a doctor's warning that salt was a major culprit and caffeine a minor one, I almost completely eliminated both substances. For a while. Then the same gravitational pull toward moderation that rules my running went to work on my appetite. It pulled me back to the lifelong habit of avoiding almost nothing while not indulging too heavily in anything.

I'm not a vegetarian. I eat all kinds of meat except lamb (which tastes to me the way a sheep smells). But a 16-ounce hunk of steak would last a week in our house, and a Big Mac would feed my wife and me for a couple of days.

Dick Beardsley

© Photo Run/Victah Sailer

We're not talking here about a dietary item as such, but something more serious. Beardsley stumbled into drug problems, as reported in the February 1997 *Running Commentary*.

In a kinder world Dick Beardsley, who turned 40 last March, would now be setting masters running records. In real life his only record is criminal. Technically what he did—and admitted to—is a crime, though the damage done is only to himself and those closest to him. But the Dick Beardsley I've known has a personality that's as far as could be from criminal. His was the desperate act of a man in constant pain.

The first time I met Dick, he was in pain. He joked onstage about tripping over a dog and hurting a knee. He already had a history of knee problems, starting when a cow had kicked him. Later Dick's troubles grew more serious. They weren't just interrupting his running anymore but threatening his life. It wasn't fair that so many bad things could happen to such a good guy: a farm accident that almost ripped off a leg, a car wreck with his family that left him with chronic back problems, then being hit in the head by a truck's side mirror while running, and finally hurting his back and head again in another auto accident.

Then came the shocking news. The headline read: "Beardsley Pleads Guilty to Felony Drug Charge." No, he wasn't using performance-enhancers or street drugs. And no, he wasn't selling. Dick was charged with forging prescriptions for painkillers that he used himself. He was just desperately trying to get through his days. He pleaded guilty. The prosecutor took Dick's history into account while recommending the minimum sentence of a fine, probation, and community service, and treatment for his drug dependence. His friends—and he has more of us than he may remember right now—

> hope that he finds the help he needs now to ease this new pain along with all the old ones. We want him to reclaim some of the joy he once knew and shared with us.
>
> Dick Beardsley said later in 1997: "Right now my focus is getting through my treatment, but you're never done with it. It's an ongoing thing. I'm hoping something positive can come from this. I'm hoping I can perhaps get out and talk to young people about drug addiction."

I'm not a nutritional extremist in either direction. Taking too much of anything isn't my way, and taking too little is a problem that quickly self-corrects. For instance, I wouldn't cut my fat to the 10 percent limit that Dean Ornish, MD (or Nathan Pritikin before him) recommends. This would mean dropping all meats and most other fats from my diet. I'd constantly hear from my rebelling body. I'd feel deprived.

But I can get by with about 20 percent fat, which is about half of what the typical American eats. It's also much less than I ate before moderating, and still my cholesterol has dropped from borderline high to normal. The fat model works in other ways. I can cut down in certain ways without cutting out.

I'm a sugar addict, for instance. I didn't try to get off the stuff cold-turkey but did reduce it by, say, adding only one spoonful to my breakfast cereal instead of two. I can eat a sugar-bomb dessert once a day rather than two or three times.

My daily dose of salt is now neither absent nor excessive. My blood pressure has moderated. The lessons in all this are two:

1. Cut down, not out.
2. Eat just about anything, just not too much of it.

Comment on the first guideline: I'm into moderation, not deprivation. When I feel deprived, that could be my body's way of telling me it craves something necessary. Comment on the second guideline: There are a few specific exceptions here that cause strong reactions (alcohol is one, caffeine less so). But I can, and do, eat and drink almost anything else—moderately, and occasionally not.

Once in a while I'll go off the wagon and onto a food binge. That's okay too. Some wise person once said, "Practice all things in moderation—including moderation."

10

Adding to the Diet

Lean away from the fatty proteins (beef, cheese, nuts)

and toward the leaner varieties (chicken, yogurt, soy).

Consume carbos as the fuel of choice. Obey the

gravitational pull toward balanced eating.

THINK TO DRINK

Weird ailments are the norm for us runners. I thought I'd heard them all, but here was a new one. Marc Bloom wrote in his *Harrier* magazine about Julia Stamps, at the time a star-crossed high school star who sometimes won big but also occasionally fell hard. (She collapsed in the 1995 and 1996 National Cross-Country Championships.)

"She has fixed a weird health problem that resulted from too much water intake and had something to do with her collapse and DNF at the [1995] Nationals," wrote Bloom. "Now she's drinking no more than three 1.5-liter bottles of water per day, half her previous intake."

Stamps drank too much. But I'd guess that most of you have the opposite problem. You probably don't drink enough water. I didn't until my inner-ear injury flared up. While I was being tested for this condition, the doctor said, "You might be chronically dehydrated. Are you drinking at least eight glasses of water a day?"

I told him of my reasonably heavy drinking. I had several cups of tea each morning. Afternoons I switched to sweetened Snapple iced tea, then back to the hot stuff at night. "None of that counts," said the doctor. "The caffeine and sugar act as diuretics, and they actually count against your fluid intake. For every sweetened or caffeinated drink you take, you need two glasses of water to make up for the loss."

By taking in only a couple of glasses of plain water each day, I was in chronic debt. My most obvious result was the inner-ear problem. Dehydration wasn't its only cause (a high-sugar diet also contributed), but drinking more water did give cheap and safe relief.

Old habits changed quickly. For 20 years I'd fueled my morning writing stint with hot, black, caffeine-rich tea. I switched to herbal and decaf varieties. Gone instantly was the beloved Snapple, which I'd downed at the rate of two to four glasses every afternoon since the product came on the market. Snapple delivered the same triple whammy—caffeine, sugar, and fluid drain—to my delicate inner ears that Pepsi, Coke, or my long-gone favorite Dr Pepper would have.

Now I even avoided most fruit juices. Their labels promise enough sugar to speed up the water loss. My doctor's nurse advised keeping a "yuppie water bottle" nearby all day. I now have one in the office and carry another in the car, and try to remember to drain them both every day.

So, you might ask, what does this have to do with you? Nothing if you already know what I've been so slow to learn about drinking needs—or if you have the Julia Stamps urge to drink too much. But if you're having problems as attention grabbing as my ear disorder—or subtle ones with heat regulation, digestion, or energy—check your water intake.

How many glasses a day do you drink, and are any of those canceled with coffee, alcohol, tea, or sugar drinks? If the first answer is "less than eight" and the second is "yes," drink up.

LEAN ON PROTEIN

My attempt to regain balance took a happy turn after a year of changing my eating habits to accommodate the inner-ear problem. I cut down on sugar and salt, tanked up on water, and ate more and smaller meals. This all helped relieve the symptoms.

Now trained to eat five or more times a day, I still hadn't learned to plan ahead. I was driving far from home when time came for an afternoon meal. I'd packed no food in the van and carried only $1 in my pocket. A fast-food outlet advertised 99-cent hamburgers, and the drive-through lane pulled me in. I devoured this cholesterol bomb, thinking that eating it quickly would cause less damage—and guilt. Afterward my head felt steadier, sooner than it had from taking any drug or from making any other diet change.

Before thinking that Burger King has enlisted a new addict, let me assure you it wasn't just a craving for fatty beef that this Whopper satisfied. It was a need for more protein—in its many and often healthier forms—than I'd let myself eat lately. As the son of a pig farmer, I grew up feasting on meat two or more times a day— if not our own product, then the beef or chicken of neighbors. Supplementing this were plenty of eggs and milk.

Over the decades, though, my protein eating dipped dramatically. I bought into the runner-wisdom that carbos are king and fat is fatal. In the 1990s I've worked at staying lean inside and out. This meant keeping my cholesterol and weight in check, which meant cutting fat, which meant eating less protein. I cut way down on meat of all kinds, stopped drinking milk and eating ice cream, ate little cheese and few eggs. Protein became a side dish instead of the main course it had long been. My intake must have fallen off by at least half in the 1990s.

After the Burger King episode, a nutrition writer from an earlier era whispered at me from her grave to reread her book. Adelle Davis published *Let's Get Well* in 1965. I'd read it then, looking for diet miracles that would translate immediately into better racing times. Finding none, I forgot Davis. Now she spoke to me again, this time about basic health. I listened as she explained that one treatment for my condition is "a diet rich in high-quality protein" (and also low in refined carbohydrates). After reading this advice, I scrambled a couple of eggs for breakfast.

More praise for protein appeared this spring in the online *Runner's World*. The item was unsigned and the source of data uncredited, but its message supported what experience was telling me: "As a runner you need more protein than the average Joe. That's because exercise causes some of your amino acids to be used for energy rather than to build protein (their usual job). This alone boosts protein needs by 25 percent. Muscle damage caused by a tough workout or race also increases protein needs, as new proteins are necessary to repair small tears in the muscle fibers. A safe recommendation for runners is to get between 0.50 and 0.72 grams of protein per pound of body weight."

I'd never counted these grams but surely had fallen far below the recommended minimum of 70 a day. That's more than a half-pound of meat (which averages about eight protein grams per ounce) or its equivalent from other sources. Now I'm eating more protein and feeling better for it. I still lean away from the fatty varieties (beef, cheese, nuts) and toward the leaner varieties (chicken, yogurt, soy), and consume carbos as the fuel of choice. I'm simply obeying the gravitational pull back toward balanced eating—which seems also to put my head in better balance.

MINERAL RICHES

I've learned more about high blood pressure in the last few years than I ever cared to know. Turns out that cutting salt (see chapter 9) wasn't the simple answer I hoped it would be.

Mike Lundgren, a running friend of mine who works with a cardiac-rehab program in Kansas City, noted that sodium isn't the only mineral in the BP equation. "A low-sodium diet, coupled with a high-potassium diet (fruits and veggies), may be even more effective," he said.

Jack Scaff, MD, a Honolulu cardiologist, added, "Sodium doesn't bear the strong relationship to hypertension that we thought it did. As a matter of fact, only about 30 percent of people are salt sensitive. Nevertheless, when athletes run, sweating is mandatory, urine production ceases, and the sweat glands literally become the 'kidneys of the skin.' The sweat glands are notably less efficient than the kidneys in maintaining serum electrolyte balance. When a hypertensive individual embarks upon a low-salt diet and exercises (with its attendant sweating), the individual is forced to lose potassium and magnesium through the skin."

The final and most convincing arguments to up my intake of other minerals came in from *Health* magazine. David McCarron of Oregon Health Sciences University told writer David Sharp that deficits of other minerals—and not overdoses of salt—may be the major culprit in high BP. McCarron named calcium, potassium, and magnesium.

"If you have enough of these other minerals," he said, "staying on a normal-sodium diet actually gives you the lowest blood pressure. Restricting your sodium intake appears to somehow impair the ability of these other minerals to keep your blood pressure low."

How to get enough: "It's almost a no-brainer," said McCarron. "You just have to eat three or four servings of fruits and vegetables each day—which means a salad at lunch and dinner, and a piece of fruit in the morning and later as a snack. If you also have three glasses of skim milk, you're there."

I probably have no problem with the potassium and magnesium. My fresh-food-fancying wife sees to that. But milk? Ah, that's the rub for me. I rarely use it in any form, having dropped most from my diet long ago because of allergic reactions. Based on the advice above, though, I've taken to raiding Barbara's stash of yogurt (which, unlike other dairy foods, I can tolerate). It can't hurt and might help.

CARBO RELOADING

In the early 1970s the first stories came out about carbohydrate loading. Depletion runs and pasta dinners quickly became required rituals before races. They still are. But only now are we seeing that carbo reloading after races might benefit us even more than loading up in advance. The last pre-event supper now appears to help us less than the first snack afterward.

One possible reason: You can't add extra fuel to an already full tank—which the well-fed, well-tapered runner will have before going to work. That work drains the tank, which eagerly sucks up fuel as quickly as you can supply it after a race or hard workout. Carbos, which convert to glycogen, provide the most accessible fuel for running. They also speed recovery.

David Costill, PhD, the sport's senior researcher, has said that the best way to recover is "tapering in reverse." Ease back into training instead of easing down, of course, but also eat more carbohydrates. Dr. Costill says he sees many runners suffering from "chronic glycogen depletion." They're energy starved because they haven't refueled properly.

So what is proper to eat, and when? Costill didn't elaborate when I talked to him several years ago. Later, valuable answers appeared. Owen Anderson, PhD, planted a clue in a *Runner's World* article about running a faster 10K. Take the carbos soon after finishing a draining effort, said Dr. Anderson. "Research has shown that's when your legs are most receptive to replenishing the glycogen stores that have been burned during training [and racing]."

What to eat? Anderson suggested choosing from among "an energy bar, 12 ounces of sports drink, a bagel, or a banana and a cup of fruit yogurt." How soon to eat? Anderson draws his advice from studies done at the University of Texas, Austin. Researchers there suggested that best results come from snacking within a half-hour after running.

That timing can be a problem. Your sports drink might not supply enough of the carbos you need, and eating solid food this soon after exercising might not sit well. One solution could be a liquid meal such as those contained in cans going by names such as Ensure or Boost. My introduction to this came through the Mead Johnson product Boost, then known by its earlier name, Results.

I tried Results while visiting the Okanagan International Marathon in British Columbia. The canned drink tastes like a thin milkshake. It contains a three-to-one ratio of carbohydrate to protein. This mix apparently gives a quick energy boost. University of Texas research shows the carbo-protein blend to work better

Kenneth Cooper

Dr. Cooper led millions of people into running with his early writings. Later he wrote increasingly about diet, as this December 1994 *Running Commentary* piece shows.

Courtesy of Cooper Aerobics Center

The growing list disturbed him. George Sheehan, Fred Lebow, and Sy Mah—all dead from cancer in recent years. Steve Scott and Mark Conover, young Olympians who'd survived cancer scares this year. The doctor wondered: Could there be a link between the hard running they did and the disease they contracted? Giving the question a scientific look, he concluded that it was at least possible. His latest book came with his strongest don't-overdo warning yet.

If anyone but Dr. Kenneth Cooper had issued this warning, it might not have earned a reply here. I might have written it off as the uninformed bleat of another antiexerciser. But Dr. Cooper has built his career around aerobic activity. He's also a careful researcher who won't make any statement without proof to back it up, and one who won't hide unpleasant facts.

Cooper is a former trackman and marathoner whose studies show that low mileage gives the best cardiovascular benefits with the least muscular-skeletal risk. Now he has found disturbing evidence that overexercising might weaken the immune system. This in turn could open the way to the diseases that we think running prevents.

His latest book explores this connection. Dr. Kenneth H. Cooper's *Antioxidant Revolution* (Thomas Nelson Publishers) puts a positive spin on the subject, saying that a combination of gentle aerobic exercise and certain dietary supplements may "delay the signs of aging, and reduce the risks of cancer and heart disease." The diet advice represents a major turnaround for Cooper. He once wrote, "If you exercise, you don't have to worry about diet." He now recommends—and takes—a daily "antioxidant cocktail" of vitamins C (500 milligrams) and E (400 international units), plus beta-carotene (25,000 IU). Cooper says these substances counteract the effects of free radicals. These are unstable oxygen molecules implicated in dozens of medical problems, and overexercising apparently releases the free radicals in excessive amounts.

So how much exercise is too much? Cooper has said for years, "If you're running more than 15 miles a week, you're running for some reason other than health." Some exercise is good, he warns, but more isn't necessarily better. "Listen to your body. Is it training or straining?"

than either of the nutrients alone. Tests with three different solutions, taken right after workouts, all increased postexercise levels of muscle glycogen. The gains:

- Protein drink, 30 percent.

- Carbohydrate drink, 103 percent.

- Carbo-protein drink, 142 percent.

Research findings don't always translate into on-the-road benefits. To know how the product really works, we must hear stories from people who have tried it. John Keston, who holds the world over-70 record for the marathon, tried Results for the first time after the Okanagan Marathon. "I can't say the drink is wholly responsible," said Keston the day after he ran 3:02. "But I feel much better than I usually do right after a marathon." Two weeks later he ran another one—in 3:03. Two weeks after that he ran yet another—in 3:07. Keston got these results (with a small *r*) by reloading and recovering quickly between marathons.

PART

Best Days

© Ken Lee

11

Counting Up
the Races

Training is, by definition, preparation for racing. You

train now to race better later. But the reverse can also

be true. You can use the racing as training.

FAST EDDY

Reno, Nevada, calls itself "The Biggest Little City in the World." Eddy Hellebuyck didn't mind the Reno Air 15K race announcer calling him the world's biggest little runner. Hellebuyck (say "Hell-a-book") must put on his Nikes to stand 5 1/2 feet tall. He must down several of Reno's all-you-can-eat meals to reach 120 pounds. Yet his size belies his strength. Few runners anywhere compete more often or better than this Belgian.

Pick almost any weekend, then check the results in *Running Stats* or *Race Results Weekly*. You're likely to find his name. He ran six high-quality marathons in the 15 months ending in April 1996. The last of those races, London, was the fastest at 2:11:53. It also put him on Belgium's Olympic team, a first for him. His country only sent five track athletes to Atlanta.

He lives in Albuquerque with his U.S.-born wife Shawn and their son Jordan, rents a second home to visiting athletes, and advises several of them. Eddy came to Reno simply because he loves to race, but admitted to overracing at times. "I was a very wild guy at one time," he told John Trent of the Reno *Gazette-Journal*. "I have a lot of talent, but I probably enjoyed running too many races. I never raced fresh." He added, "I used to be lazy." That was one reason he raced so often: It assured him a hard workout.

Having some of the best runners from Europe and Africa living nearby has changed his ways somewhat. His housemates and renters have included Peter Whitehead of Britain, fourth-place marathoner at the 1995 World Championships; Olympic track medalist Khalid Skah, and top Kenyan road racer Benson Masya. "Since I've brought these people to my homes," said Eddy, "I've been able to see how professional they are, how focused they are in their approach. Before, if I was tired or having a bad day I would just jog through the workout. Now if I go out with some of the Kenyans and I have a bad day, they'll kick my butt."

His wife Shawn, herself a runner, interjected here, "If he cuts his run short, I ask him, 'What are you doing home so soon?' He's a professional, like a plumber who can't afford to stop early because he doesn't feel so good that day."

Having great athletes living nearby also reminds Eddy that they're human. They, too, get hurt and fall out of shape. He recalled a visit from Skah. "He couldn't even run seven-minute miles. Late

Eddy Hellebuyck (center).

that summer he came in second in the World Championships 10,000. Considering how far he had come from March, it was an amazing performance. You learn from these people that if you work hard, you can do it."

RACE TO TRAIN

Training is, by definition, preparation for racing. You train now to race better later. But the reverse can also be true. You can use the racing as training.

Eddy Hellebuyck does it. This is the method behind his racing mania. "There's no way I can push myself as hard in training as I can in a race," he told me during our visit at the Reno Air 15K. Maria Trujillo, winning woman at Reno and another megaracer, added, "I use my short races as training." Nowhere else does the excitement run as high. Nowhere are the stresses so specific.

In an Olympic year, runners make the mistake of limiting their racing. They'll "save the big one for when it counts," then peak as they race more often after the Games. Races supply the final sharpness that might not come any other way. This is an experience that training can't duplicate. Look at the results of one year's world-ranked track men and women:

- 1500m—best time in the fifth big race of the season at that distance or the mile.

- Men's steeple, women's 3000m, and men's and women's 5000m—best time in fourth race.

- 10,000m—best time in second race.

Of the 80 rankers, only 15 ran their fastest in their first serious race of the year. Nine of these were in the 10,000m, where racing opportunities are limited and they surely competed earlier in shorter events.

I certainly don't compare myself with them, but the same forces work at my much slower pace. One of my best racing seasons started with a 4:45 mile. Eight weeks and as many mile races later, the time had dropped to 4:22—with no other change in the training. More than a quarter-century later, I made a brief return to the track. Times were much slower by then, yet they still improved by 30 seconds during a series of weekly mile races.

If races push runners to go harder than they would alone, they also make the work seem easier. Megamarathoners, those who run one a month or more, do most of their long running in the marathons—where they have running mates, drink stations, traffic control, and split times—and stay well off PR pace. Sy Mah rarely ran longer than five miles between his marathons, which totaled 524 in his lifetime. Norm Frank, who has exceeded Mah's count, runs only once or twice—and not more than five miles—between his weekly marathons.

During one three-month period, my only runs longer than an hour were in races. In those three half-marathons the pace dropped by a full minute per mile, with no apparent increase in effort. Racing still is hard work. And it still works as training.

George Beinhorn

Some runners like to add up races by using them as training. Beinhorn does that, as told in this December 1997 *Running Commentary* article.

When ultrarunners talk technique, I listen. They're "out there," not only in distance but on the leading edge of what works. George Beinhorn is one of them. But long before escalating his distances, he was a coworker of mine at *Runner's World*. Now in his mid-50s and living in the San Francisco Bay area, George runs ultras by the dozens each year. He explained how and why in a recent flurry of e-mails between us.

In the first he wrote, "I've recently adopted a new system of ultra training: just two or three runs per week. All you need to do is two or three ultras per month and a little jogging. I got the idea for my training methods from Suzi Thibeault, who has run more 100s than any other woman. While running with her a little in a race, I asked her how she trained." She told George, "I don't. I just run two or three ultras every month and maybe jog some one day a week." Then he talked with Eric Robinson, who had run about 26 hours at Western States that year. Robinson said, "I don't really train. I just run races"—again two or three times a month.

Not long ago George had felt frustration with ultras, "thinking I had to run high mileage to improve and being prevented from doing so by my job. All's well now, though." He told of a friend who was training 120 miles a week to prepare for the Western States 100 and mentioned this to Jim King. "Why are you killing yourself running high mileage?" asked King. "I won Western States three times and never ran more than 70 or 80 miles a week."

No ultras are on my calendar. But I see the value of this advice in the lesser distances where most of us reside. George Beinhorn's report suggests that high mileage, and especially everyday running, is overrated. Everyone—marathoners down to 5Kers—could be placing too much faith in mile-counting and run-streaking. Big days may be more productive and satisfying than big weeks. We might make good days better by running more distance on them and putting more time between them.

RACING COUNTS

Writers on running sometimes fail in the simplest of writing tasks. They don't take careful notes on their own running. George Sheehan promised himself to start a diary someday. He never did. Facts-and-figures writing wasn't his style. He could recall everything he ever felt about a race run 20 years ago, but couldn't tell you his exact time from his next-to-last one. George probably ran more than 1000 races. But he couldn't have guessed within 100 of the true count, and didn't care.

Hal Higdon spoke for his fellow writer when he said, "Counting never seemed as important as doing." Hal's own record-keeping had been casual. "Over the years when people have asked how many marathons I've run, I've answered 100," he said. This number sounded so neat that Hal had used it since the early 1980s.

As a footnote to his book on the 100th running of Boston, Hal tried to recreate his own marathon history. He searched incomplete diaries and hazy memories. "I discovered I am somewhat short of a hundred," he told me in 1995. "The number is somewhere between 92 and 95." He pinned down the exact count, then timed the count so he would run number 100 at Boston 1996.

Hal had an imminent goal, which he reached. Mine remains so distant that it's more a vague wish than a goal. Running 1000 lifetime races would be nice. Not many runners have documented this many. Sy Mah surely did, as his marathons alone totaled 524. Johnny Kelley long since ran his 1000th race. But more people have run sub-four-minute miles than have raced this often. It isn't a feat requiring great talent, or even great effort in each race. What it mainly takes is time: almost 20 years of weekly races, or longer if the count adds up at a slower rate.

If my early pace had held up, I would have passed this milestone at a rather young age. I was halfway there by age 30. But then the count slowed to a race-every-month-or-less crawl. I took another seven years to reach my 600th race—and then quit counting. Like Hal Higdon, I talked in round numbers. For the previous 10 years, my bio had listed "about 700" races. Hal's story prodded me to update my count. To my delight, the 700th race arrived at the 1994 George Sheehan Classic. Megaracer George would have been pleased for me, but still mystified as to why anyone would bother counting.

I agree that the number alone means little. Running races only to add to the total would be a silly exercise in mathematics. But each race also stores memories. I once thought the best racing ones would be numerical: How far, how fast, how high the finish? But they aren't. The value of the race count is the accumulation of memorable experiences. These center on the places I wouldn't otherwise have gone and the people I wouldn't otherwise have seen. I can cover my eyes and point to any line on the lengthy accounting of races. Few facts appear there, but lasting impressions of that day flash back to life instantly and in rich detail.

I'd love to pick up the pace of race counting again. This would not be an attempt to speed progress toward a distant round-number goal. (At today's rate, 1000 wouldn't arrive before my 80th birthday.) More racing would give me that much more to remember. I can think of no finer way to spend the rest of a running lifetime than by counting up races.

RACING STATES

On a trip to Los Angeles, I fell into step with a runner named Morgan Behr. He mentioned during the hour of running conversation that he belonged to the Century Club, members of which must have visited at least 100 countries. My wife Barbara, with more than 40 nations in her passport, itches to become a Centurion someday. But I'm not ready to join her world travels. I still have too much of the United States to see before venturing abroad.

I love this country. This isn't a political statement, but an expression of fondness for the vast and varied land and its people. Occasionally I read about runners who've logged a marathon in every state. I envy their travels.

Ed Burnham of Kansas City is the oldest to do this. *Master Pieces* magazine reports that Burnham waited until age 70 to run his first marathon. At 75 he completed his national tour—a marathon in every state—in Mississippi. Paul Reese (see chapter 6) knows how big an accomplishment this is, because it has eluded him. Reese, who's two years older than Burnham, has covered more of this country on foot than anyone his age. At 80 he reached his goal of crossing every state.

Paul thought about and vetoed making a national marathon sweep. "The running would have been the easy part of it," he says. "The accomplishment would have been in the logistics—scheduling the races, staying healthy enough to run them, and being able to afford the time and money to travel to them." He adds that "I once laid out a program of running 10 marathons a year for five consecutive years to hit all the states. After I succeeded in setting up the schedule—and that was no easy task—I looked at the cost of airfare, hotels, and time, and as a result retreated."

The Burnham-Reese discussion led to a count of my marathon states. The total is a paltry seven, and I might not even hit double figures before the century turns. But adding up states will never be my goal as a marathoner. My plan in this event is to add special experiences—like visiting the most spectacular courses or areas where I've lived, and these leave out most of the states.

Counting marathons did raise other questions: In how many states have I run races of any length? And how possible is it to cover them all? I've already raced in 35 states (as well as four Canadian provinces, but in only one country that doesn't border the United States). The remaining states sit in clusters—several in New England, a few in the mid-Atlantic, a couple in the Deep South, a set in the northern Rockies. Four brief flurries of driving and racing would complete my tour of the United States. This could easily happen before the century turns. What better way to see the country I love most?

12

Rerunning the Best Races

Now the races are more social than athletic. There's
much to be said for this approach, but the results
aren't as memorable as when the stakes are high and
the efforts are full.

RACES TO REMEMBER

Bob Wischnia at *Runner's World* faxed a request for an entry in a writing contest he was organizing. To prompt my thinking, he talked about what led to a story he planned to compile. "Several months ago in the middle of the worst race of my life," he wrote, "I began wondering why I even bother running races. I'm not any good, but for some reason that doesn't matter. I never beat anyone, but that doesn't bother me. The concept of breaking personal records no longer motivates me. I mean, nobody cares if I run 39:27 or 42:27 [for a 10K, which I'd guess is the range of his PR and the recent PW]. I'm not even sure I care."

"Wish" (as his coworkers call him) was too tough on himself, or maybe he was just exercising his writer's gift for exaggeration. Not any good, never beats anyone? Even at his worst he travels at better than seven minutes a mile. Anyway, back to his tale: "But something must drive me as well as many of our readers to run races. Which is a back-alley approach to a story we will be attempting." He would title it "My Most Memorable Race." Not just his, he quickly added, but ours. He asked the entire staff for entries. "What's memorable?" asked Wish as he began listing guidelines. "It depends on you. It could be your first race, worst race, best race, favorite race."

My choice as most memorable wasn't a first race or a fastest race. It wasn't a Boston Marathon or an NCAA Cross-Country Championship. It was . . . well, we'll get to that later (see "One That Got Away" later in this chapter). That choice wasn't easy. I had a hard time even cutting to 10 finalists. They ranged across most of the ground that Bob Wischnia wanted his writing team to cover: big and small races, track and cross-country races, first and longest races. Each memorable race taught me lessons. Each was, in some big or small way, a course-changing event. Some made me feel proud when I needed that. Some humbled me when I needed that.

None of the 10 most memorable races is less than 25 years old. I haven't stopped racing since then, although the count has slowed as much as my pace. But it's hard for these current events to compete with memories stored up at a time when everything was new and oh-so-important. Now the races are more social and nostalgic than athletic. There's much to be said for this approach too, but the results aren't as memorable as when the stakes are high and the efforts are full.

Joan Benoit Samuelson

© Photo Run/Victah Sailer

No one has enjoyed a finer best race than Samuelson. Hers was a gold-medal performance in the first Olympic Marathon for women. I talked with her 10 years later for a July 1994 *Running Commentary* article.

There's no one I respect more in this sport. But that didn't stop me from elbowing her out of the way to speak first at the Manitoba Marathon. "This is the only time I'll ever get to lead Joan Benoit Samuelson," I told the brunch crowd in Winnipeg. I finished first, then she stood to speak.

I hadn't seen Joan since 1984, her greatest year. Her running has been quiet the past few years, but time has been good to her legend. She's still the second-fastest marathoner in world history, nine years after running 2:21:21, and still the best American by five minutes. Joan might be even more admirable for what she hasn't done. She hasn't tried to be a professional gold-medalist, living up to and cashing in on a bigger-than-life image. She doesn't color her hair, which is now more gray than its earlier black. She doesn't hide behind makeup the lines of her 37 years. She makes few endorsements. She travels sparingly, preferring the life of a mother and wife.

She came to Canada only on the condition that the family could travel with her on Father's Day weekend. She chose to enter the family fun run with husband Scott, six-year-old Abigail and four-year-old Anders instead of running a longer race alone. "My children are my focus now," she told the crowd. "They demand and receive much of my energy. I used to look at my watch and worry about my splits. Now I look at the watch and worry about getting back in time to pick up Abby and Anders."

At the time of her daughter's birth, Joan was asked, "When are you going to give her a pair of running shoes?" She replied, "When she asks for them." Abby now has the shoes but runs in them only if she chooses. The girl without her two front teeth still doesn't know that Joan Samuelson is anyone but Mom. Abby came home from school after talking about the Winter Games and asked, "Do we know any Olympians?" (Joan Samuelson realized a goal in 1996 by running the Olympic Trials Marathon with her children watching.)

DISTANT REPLAYS

Every race is a memory made. So with a lifetime race count numbering 700-plus, I had a lot of memories to sort through when asked for the most memorable. Before naming my most memorable race, let me talk of the other nine contenders. I don't try to rank them in order of memorability, only in the order run:

• **First high school mile**. I made a rookie mistake, starting too fast and not lasting beyond the first turn of the second lap. I might have stopped forever right there, but my coach wouldn't let me. "You owe me one," was what Dean Roe said. That's all he had to say. One more race led to another, then dozens, then hundreds.

• **Last steeplechase**. In the first one, I'd finished almost a lap behind Hal Higdon, today the sport's senior writer but then among the country's best steeplers. The second race brought me together with another high schooler. We came to the final barrier together. My form was slightly less ragged than his, and I won by a step. Mike Manley went on to make an Olympic team in this event. I never ran it again.

• **Last high school race**. I faced Don Prichard in the mile at the state meet. He'd won easily a few weeks earlier at the Drake Relays. Our state race wasn't close either. To my amazement and Don's, I put five seconds between us while lowering my PR by three. I thought this was the start of great races to come in college and beyond. In fact, my racing career peaked that day at age 17.

- **First national championship race**. The NCAA Cross Country meet wasn't memorable for the running. Drake's team wound up in midpack, and so did I (see chapter 13). No, this weekend was historic for another reason. Our travel day was to be a Friday, November 22, 1963. The race was delayed by a day, and we watched John F. Kennedy's funeral from a motel room in Michigan. A running event was never as important after that.

- **First marathon**. Where else to start but Boston? It was the only U.S. marathon that counted then, and you could still enter there without earning a qualifying time elsewhere. My longest run had been 20 miles and its pace only eight-minute miles. So I figured to go the extra distance at the same rate and finish in $3\frac{1}{2}$ hours. But I hadn't counted on the magic of Boston. My time, 2:49, stuck as a permanent PR.

- **Longest relay**. The 24-hour relay figured to be a marathon's worth of mile runs, about one per hour, so I thought of trying to hold marathon pace. The team wouldn't let me off that easily. My mates clicked off miles in the mid-fives. I couldn't let them down, so mine averaged 5:38. A race has magical powers, and so does teamwork. Put the two together and they lead to some truly memorable days.

- **Longest race**. One hundred miles would have been far outside my frame of reference. Even a marathon usually seemed too long. But then I heard about taking walking breaks to extend the distance range. Why not put this trick to the ultimate test? I failed in one sense; I dropped out at 70 miles. But this was success in another way: almost $2\frac{1}{2}$ times longer than ever before, and my first proof that walking breaks work.

- **First Eugene race**. Even in 1971 this was the mecca of our sport. I first visited Eugene for the National Championship Marathon. The race itself was memorable for several reasons: running the last five miles barefoot after my shoes failed, finishing lower than ever before or since, and ending at Hayward Field as the mile (with Jim Ryun and Steve Prefontaine) was playing to the usual full house. Imagine living here, I thought then. Ten years later, after three more scouting missions at Eugene's series of Olympic Trials, this became my home.

- **Last fast marathon**. Well, that is if breaking three hours counts as "fast." It didn't seem so then but it seems faster to me all

the time. The scene was the 1972 Avenue of the Giants in northern California (see chapter 22). Courses come no better than this. It features trees as big around as houses and as tall as skyscrapers. Running through this forest of redwoods was as quiet and spiritual as passing through a cathedral. What a place to peak out!

ONE THAT GOT AWAY

We were pretty good. Understand that this wasn't the big time but the second-lowest level of high school running in one of the smallest states. But by the standards of Iowa in those years, we had outstanding track and cross-country teams. At a school reunion 35 years later, I reminisced with old teammates about all we'd done back then. And I relived the one that got away because I'd forgotten how to count to four.

South Page was a new school in the fall of 1959. Three towns had folded their schools into one. The quickest way to put old rivalries aside and get to know each other was as sports teammates. I joined two teams that first fall, cross-country and football. We practiced for the two sports at opposite ends of the school day. We once ran a state meet on a Saturday morning, then jumped in cars and drove halfway across Iowa to play a football game that night.

Our team won the state cross-country title that season with one of our scorers doubling as the football quarterback. Norm Johnston went on to become an All-American hurdler at Iowa State University and then to come within three places of making the 1968 Olympic decathlon team. I was a member of two more state championship teams in South Page's second year as a school. These joined my half-dozen individual titles.

We enjoyed many successes, some of them now half forgotten. But all these years later I still dwell more on a spectacular failure. It was the dumbest in a multitude of dumb moves I've made as a runner. I hit bottom for dumbness in the school's first-ever track meet. The State Indoor at Iowa City was the first time any of us had ever run under a roof.

Norm Johnston had done his part, giving South Page enough points in the two hurdle races and high jump to put the team in the title race. I'd won the mile. A victory in the medley relay would win the meet for the new school. I took the baton for the final half-mile in good position to win. Focusing only on the shirt backs in front of me, my plan was to spurt ahead on the last of the four laps on this dirt track.

Striking as planned, I dashed down the homestretch in the lead. An official held up one finger, which I took to mean first place. Exiting into the chute at the end of the track, I felt no finish tape. The same official shouted, "No, you're not done! One more lap!" I made a U-turn and rejoined the chase, but too late. We scored no points in the relay. We took home no team trophy.

It's human nature to dwell more on dumb mistakes than on successes. The worst mistakes can also be the best teachers. I learned that night to count to four. And I learned that letting down the team feels 20 times worse than disappointing only myself.

A LOVE THAT LASTS

Frequent correspondent Cathy Troisi responded to my apology for not getting to the Boston Marathon and missing our planned meeting there by saying, "You didn't miss anything." This wasn't cynicism on her part. Anything but. Cathy loves Boston. She said, "You didn't miss anything because once you've run Boston, it is always a part of you, and you share in marathon day from wherever you are."

How true. I never really miss a Boston Marathon, even from 3000 miles away. Boston is forever memorable to anyone who has run there. But it's especially so for me because it was my first marathon. Like first love, no matter how it turned out, that first marathon always stays with you because the experience was new and extra special. You rarely see an old lover after the romance cools. But Boston lets you revisit and rekindle the flame each April.

I was at home in Oregon this Patriots Day. I marked the day by refreshing the affection from afar with this love letter in my diary:

Today, as in every year since 1967, I run the Boston Marathon. I've only been back three times since the first to run there for real, but I'm always there—rejoining the marathoners in a line a hundred years and hundreds of thousands of runners long. The media hookup by way of TV, newspapers, and now the Internet is incidental. It deals almost entirely with the otherworldly characters up front. They interest me less as the gap between us in age and pace grows wider.

Then again, we were never that close. Even at 23 I lagged more than a half-hour behind the leaders. The race covered nationally was never the one I knew. It's even less so now. Doesn't matter, though. I don't need these news reports to connect me to Boston. I have a set of mental pictures, as clear now as when they were first shot. They tell me exactly what the runners a continent away are doing this morning.

- They woke up and checked the weather at dawn as I got up for a middle-of-the-night pit stop.
- They board the buses to the start as dawn reaches the West Coast and I sit down to write this page.
- They will overcrowd Hopkinton as I finish writing and go for a routine morning run.
- They will begin lining up as I eat breakfast and read about their would-be leaders in the morning paper.
- They will start the marathon as I sit down to work.
- They will welcome the cheers in Wellesley as I take a midmorning tea-and-pee break.
- They who run my old pace will finish as I stop for lunch.

- They who run my current pace (that's you, Cathy Troisi) will finish as I mow the lawn in early afternoon.

While my day at home will be mundane and its events soon forgotten, the Boston runners will spend the same amount of time making unforgettable magic. This day will never end for them. They'll be in Boston with me every Patriots Day from now on.

13

Worrying About the Race

Don't be afraid of the fear. It's normal and even

helpful—the mind's way of getting the body ready to

do something big.

THE FEAR FACTOR

High school runners don't often cross paths with me. But one cross-country season I struck up e-mail correspondence with an Ohio boy going by the online name "Joedogg." He told an anguished tale of nervousness that spilled over into panic. Joedogg's track times as a high school junior had ranged from 1:59 in the 800 to 9:38 in the 3200. This cross-country season, though, he'd suddenly found himself unable to exploit his talents because of his fears.

His first note asked for advice on staying calm in the days and hours before his state-qualifying meet. Not yet knowing how seriously agitated he was, I tossed off some general tips: Don't be afraid of the fear. It's normal and even helpful—the mind's way of getting the body ready to do something big.

Joedogg wrote back after that week's meet. Nothing I'd told him had helped. His race had been a near disaster. "My team and I qualified for the state meet," he said, "but I had a very subpar race." He fought his nerves with mixed success. He slept well the night before but woke up shaky.

"The nerves seemed to go away once I got on the bus and was around my teammates," he noted. "I tried to focus on the task at hand and got nervous again. We started our warm-up for the race, and it all went away. Then I started to put on my racing shoes, and it all hit me. I thought, 'This could be my last high school race.' My stomach started getting really upset. It stayed that way as I walked to the starting line. At one point I even had to stop and crouch over to compose myself."

The butterflies flew away when Joedogg saw his dad and some friends. He felt reasonably calm when the race began. Then he found himself buried in the pack during the opening rush, and he panicked. He surged a half-dozen times in the first mile to pass people. His mile time was 5:02. Then he slipped to 5:32 in the second mile and tried to accelerate. Nothing there. Joedogg's third mile took almost seven minutes. His final 5K time was his slowest in two years.

"Two people had to hold me up in the chute, then I had to go to an ambulance to get oxygen," he said. "It was horrible." This time I referred him to an expert. I sent chapters from an upcoming book by Joe Newton, whose teams had won Illinois cross-country titles in 19 of his 36 years as coach.

Newton wrote, "High school kids make mountains of molehills, getting so nervous that they risk psyching themselves out. We want them to be aggressive and have some nervous tension but don't want them to fall apart mentally. I'm constantly emphasizing that they don't have to get all panic-stricken. They don't need to hammer the heck out of the course or try to exceed themselves. No big breakthrough is required. They only have to run up to the potential that they've shown before. I tell them, 'Just be yourself—no more, no less.'"

Joedogg had the resilience of youth working for him. The bad memories were already fading and the anticipation growing as he wrote before the state meet, "Several people have told me that you get more nervous for a regional race because you have to qualify there for the state meet. Once you qualify, you can relax and think, 'Wow, I made it!' So I am going into the state meet with a lot of confidence, knowing that I belong here. There is no pressure. I just have to run my own race."

A week later Joedogg reported back from the state meet. He told of panic rising again in midrace. "Physically I was ready to go faster," he said, "but mentally I was afraid of dying at the end and ending up in the ambulance again."

The worst didn't happen this time. His pace held up, and he finished more than a minute faster than the week before. This time Joedogg said he didn't feel tired enough at the end. He thinks he could have gone 20 seconds faster and beaten another 35 runners. For now, though, he could take pride in putting this one demon behind him.

Alberto Salazar

Salazar's running career was as troubled as it was brilliant. He ran some astonishing races, but also compiled a depressing medical history. Just when his career seemed finished, he ran and won the world's number-one ultramarathon. The July 1994 *Running Commentary* told of his Comrades victory in South Africa.

I applaud Alberto Salazar as loudly as anyone. The more trouble he has faced and overcome, the more I've cheered. He talked of what winning Comrades meant to him in a remarkably frank interview with Ron Bellamy of the Eugene *Register-Guard*.

"A lot of people looked at me over the last 10 years—justifiably so, probably—as a punch-drunk old fighter who doesn't know when to quit," said Salazar. "I've been a crappy runner. I'd get fifth in local road races."

Salazar's once-legendary mental toughness also came back into play during the 54-mile South African race. He described his extended battle with his weaker side: "With 20 miles to go, I was ready to drop out. I was so hot and out of it, I literally just

© Photo Run/Victah Sailer

wanted to lie down on the road." His wife Molly rode along in a van. Alberto recalled thinking, "I'm going to get in that van and tell Molly that if I ever think of doing anything so stupid again in my life to slap me." He thought, "I'm no good as a runner anymore. Why keep embarrassing myself?"

But then he thought, "I drop out here, and I've already opened my mouth and said I'm running for God. What sort of example is that going to be? Everyone is going to think I'm such a head case."

Salazar wanted no personal credit for finishing and winning. "I have no sense of accomplishment on my own," he said. "It's so clear that it was a miracle, and that God pulled me through. There's no doubt in my mind where the strength came to finish the race." He added that, "in the past, running was an end in itself. Before, running was sort of my God. Now, coming around the second time, a much greater purpose is to share my faith that people should have a relationship with God. It's a pretty simple message, but it's one that I can share more if I'm running well. In this society, whoever is doing well gets the attention."

RELAXING PACE

Coach Joe Newton says the midrace breakdowns like Joedogg's in the story above are less the result of mental problems than pacing problems. The boy was a 16:30 5K runner in earlier races on this same course, now starting at 15:30 pace. "Most high school races start at breakneck speed—too fast, in my opinion," says Newton. "This leads to slowing down too much in midrace. The jackrabbit starters then turn to tortoises, slowing down radically."

When the irreversible slowdown begins and the parade of runners starts passing, the worst fears come true. The self-recriminations follow: "I'm weak-willed for not pushing harder when the pace started to slip." I've spoken those words. I remember the feelings behind them, although they're ghosts from the early 1960s.

I'd moved from being the fastest high school miler in the state to potentially the slowest cross-country runner on our college team. I had to prove myself all over again—every day in practice as well as in races. I'd go out hard in the races, only to fall apart in the middle and struggle home at the end. My mile time that year slowed by almost half a minute, my two-mile by 45 seconds, my three-mile by more than a minute.

When my freshman year ended, I quit running for the first time in four years. My nerves were worn out, and I needed time off to think about where to go from here. Was I too weak mentally to be a college runner? Maybe . . . but I'd been weak before, and had run much better than this.

A month off for reflection convinced me that I could do okay again. There was nothing wrong with me that changes in training and pacing couldn't fix. I worked up my courage to approach the coach and ask to be excused from team practices. He agreed, having already written me out of his team-scoring plans. I modified my training to a style more suited to me. But mainly I freed myself of the awful nervous tension that went with group running every day. I saved that for races, when it counted.

At the meets I spread the pace evenly over the whole distance instead of starting like a hare and finishing like a tortoise. Before, I'd tried to run 4:10 miles on 4:30 ability, or 9:00 two-miles with a 10-minute body. Now I started quietly and saved my moves for later. The moves were now there to make. They showed me how much better it feels to pass than be passed in midrace.

I set no worlds afire as a journeyman college runner. But my track times returned to where they were meant to be. After hitting bottom as a freshman cross-country runner, I scored each of the remaining years for a team that won three straight conference titles. Twice I lined up with my teammates at the NCAA Championships. The team and coach got some help from me after all—after all the fears eased and the pace moderated.

KIDS WHO CARE

Kids don't run anymore. Kids don't care about running. Kids see it as boring, a sport better suited to their parents and grandparents. That's what I'd heard for years. That's what I'd written more than once. The problem with that theory was that I hadn't checked it out by going to a high school or age-group track meet or cross-country race in all the time I'd been thinking this. I'd only seen the statistical evidence that youth performances were slipping both locally and nationally.

Then one Saturday, a rare free afternoon opened on a weekend. I had no writing begging attention, no house or yard chores to do, no kids of my own to haul anywhere. The sun shone after a rainstorm. The air had the bite of early fall to it. This was a perfect cross-country day, a day to bring out the kid in me. The best days of my youth were fall days. The best time to be a runner was cross-country season. A visit to the state high school meet in Eugene reawakened those good old times.

Two of my worst races, both NCAA Cross Country Championships, now supply some of the best memories. This meet was still so small in the 1960s that any team could enter without qualifying, and my two races there ranged from fair as a junior to poor as a senior. I was a true midpacker in 1963 as an equal number of runners led and trailed my 120th-place finish. The next fall, running on a snow-packed course that would have been perfect for cross-country skiing, I slipped 100 places lower. Back then, I cared desperately about placings and about carrying my load for the team. I thought my cross-country career had ended in dismal failure.

But as years passed and runs slowed, my outlook changed. I've come to see those two NCAA meets in particular, and cross-

country seasons in general, as my happiest and proudest running moments. It doesn't matter that I beat only 20 fellow stragglers in my last big meet. What counts was being there at all, running the open country with teammates and against the best young runners this nation had to offer then.

Those days are 30 years behind me now. But I can still go back to recall them at meets like the Oregon high school championships. I can stand beside the course, closer to these runners than is possible at track meets or road races, close enough to hear them groan and smell them sweat, close enough to see their looks of resolve and despair.

I can stand among a surprising number of fans. They came to the Eugene meet by the thousands, jamming traffic as they lined up to pay for parking. Most of these people weren't generic fans of running like me. They were family or friends who came to support one special runner.

The only one I knew was a boy named Matt. Like all other runners there, he wore a look of desperate caring about his finish position that I'd worn at his age. Matt looked downcast the last time he passed my viewing spot. He was placing much farther back and helping his team less than he'd hoped.

Nothing I could have said just then would have made him feel any better. He'll need more time before he can look back on this as one of his best days. Anyone who cares this deeply about a race will never forget it. As long as young runners keep caring this much, the sport's future is in fine shape.

PASSING INTERESTS

Aprils have been good to me. I ran my first mile one April Fool's Day and my first marathon one Patriots Day. My fastest mile and marathon came in April, three years apart. As with the fall cross-country seasons of my youth, my best memories of April don't center on what I did then, but what we did. In the Midwest, April was the month for running as relay teams.

Most of the year, members of those track teams went their own ways in many different events. Only a common singlet and a combined score linked them. In cross-country they raced together yet alone. An individual could succeed even as the team failed, and not all individuals contributed to the final score.

This really became a team sport only in a relay. Here runners competed separately yet as a single unit. The team couldn't finish unless all members carried their share of the load. Teaming up brought out the best in the individuals. It's no accident that my mile PR came while leading off a relay team where three other milers counted on me not to dig them too deep a hole.

Since college I've had few chances to run relays. Road racing is a loner sport with little tradition for teamwork. It traditionally has appealed to older, unaffiliated runners who train mostly by themselves. They race alone in the crowd, then only find old friends and make new ones afterward.

The larger races grow, the less personal they become. In response to the lost-in-the-crowd feeling of mass races, road runners have started to regroup in more sociable ways. The largest race in my home state is the Hood to Coast Relay. About 1000 teams of 12 run these 192 miles. Runners joining their first relay team fret over carrying their share of the load.

"In other races," said one woman before Hood to Coast, "you only disappoint yourself by not doing well. Here you let down 11 other people." After the race, however, this same runner called the relay her best running experience to date. She said, "I went farther and faster than I ever could have gone without team support."

Her story illustrates the two sides of teamwork. Running for a team adds a prerace concern, but multiplies the postrace joy. By giving more of yourself for the team, you get more from yourself in return. Success then tastes extra sweet when you can share it with teammates.

14

Racing the Short Distances

The shortest of road distances make ideal speedwork

for the heavy-duty racer, and it's a great place to

break in for the novice.

MY FIRST MILE

Thanks, Doc. I needed that. The doctor, in this case, is Roger Bannister. He gave me an early and essential booster shot in this sport.

Forty years later, I added my small tribute to him on the anniversary of the single most celebrated event in running history. I ran a timed mile in his honor. Most of the living world-record holders in the mile gathered with Dr. Bannister in Oxford, England, to commemorate his race of May 6, 1954. Current masters, who were babies then, raced on the historic Iffley Road track.

I celebrated from afar, just as I did when Bannister first crossed the four-minute barrier. News of his race hooked me permanently into the magic of the mile. I was only 10 years old in May 1954, and most of my memories of that time are lost in the haze of too many birthdays. This was long before I took up the habit of recording every scrap of running trivia, yet one memory is indelible. I'd heard for years from my track-fan dad of the four-minute-mile chase. I heard his happy whoop when news reached him that Bannister, a medical student from England, had just run 3:59.4.

My neighborhood gang already held track meets each spring. But we competed only in the sexy events—hurdles over window screens propped up with bricks, pole vault with a water pipe, javelin with a bamboo pole, discus with a metal plate. We did little straight-ahead running, and none lasting longer than a minute. We never timed or measured anything; we just competed.

Bannister planted the idea of running a mile for time. I thought it would be neat to run it in less than twice his time. After all, I was less than half his age. None of my buddies cared for the idea of going this far. But they agreed to help me with the measuring, timing, and pacing. Three of us took turns stepping off the distance around the home block. We averaged about a quarter-mile for this "track" that was uphill on one side and down on another.

We borrowed Dad's precious stopwatch, which he normally only brought out for real track meets. The most reliable and surehanded of the neighbor boys, the preacher's son, took charge of the timing. I enlisted pacers, as Bannister had done. Each would run in front of me for one lap around the block.

This first timed mile (or timed anything) took me seven minutes and 23 seconds. I'll never forget the time, or my first case of shin splints that resulted from this mile. The pain soon went away, but my fascination with this distance never did. Fully one-third of all my 700-plus races have been miles, and so have most of the best races.

I never thought seriously about breaking four minutes. But I did close the gap from more than 80 percent slower than that time to less than 8 percent above it. Ten years almost to the day after that first mile, I ran my fastest one. A 4:18.

I once read of an old miler, Joie Ray, running a mile on each birthday for old times' sake. He continued this practice into very old age. I can't wait a year. I still run a mile for speed at least once every week. Each one links me to a past that now reaches back more than 40 years. Thanks, Doc Bannister, for starting all this.

Eamonn Coghlan

© UPI/Corbis-Bettmann

Forty years after the first runner, Roger Bannister, broke four minutes for the mile, the first man over 40 broke that same barrier. *Running Commentary* of April 1994 reported on Coghlan's race.

It wasn't quite now-or-never for Eamonn Coghlan. But it was sooner, not later. His time to become the first sub-four-minute masters miler was running out. He had said so himself in a recent *New York Times* interview. "If I'm not going to do it this year," the Irishman had told Frank Litsky, "I'm not going to do it. It gets harder as you get older."

The four-minute barrier had turned back other great milers. Mike Boit never got in shape for a serious attempt after 40.

Illness canceled Rod Dixon's bid. Injury stopped John Walker. Coghlan had come closer than anyone, but even he had followed nature's timetable of losing a second or two per year since peaking at age 30. He'd also discovered the truism of masters running—that runners his age (41) get hurt quicker and heal slower. He nursed a chronic hamstring injury, which he called "literally a pain in the rear end."

Now his best chance had come. The injury was under control, and the conditions were right. The world's most skilled indoor miler (he still held the open record, set 11 years ago) would run on one of the world's fastest indoor tracks. The track at Harvard is eight laps to the mile, with a springy surface and wide, banked turns. He enlisted a world-class rabbit. Stanley Redwine, an 800-meter man, did his job perfectly by towing Coghlan through three quarters in just under three minutes. This left Coghlan needing to run a quarter in 60.7 or faster. He would have to do it alone.

"If I run 4:00.1 or 4:00.2," he had said, "I'll be a million miles away from 3:59.8 or 3:59.9." He was hundreds of miles from the bigtime indoor circuit he used to tread. This event came during a break in a high school meet. The kids cheered wildly for this man old enough to be their father who finished in 3:58.15.

Quibblers might protest that this wasn't an outdoor mile, that it was a patched-together event, that it was paced, that it wasn't a true masters race. Don't listen to them. Give Eamonn Coghlan full claim to one of the milestone times in running history.

HIGH-LEVEL MILE

This mile was high-level in name only. Its field wasn't large, and its winners weren't fast. The only national-class runners here were marathoners who ran with their young children on this night. The High-Level Mile took its name from a bridge that crosses the Saskatchewan River in Edmonton. This event played a minor role in the city's week-long Sports Festival, which ended with the Edmonton Marathon and Half. Nearly 1500 runners entered those races, but fewer than 100 tried the mile.

I was among them, partly because of a longtime weakness for the mile and equally for the love of running across bridges. My earliest hometown runs took me down to the Silver Bridge, south of town, and back. Memorable bridges run in marathons include the Golden

Gate in San Francisco, Bixby in Big Sur, and the many crossings in New York City. Edmonton's High-Level Bridge is the equal of any other I've run, if only because the mile race is run entirely on the bridge. Cross in one traffic-free lane, turn around and come back in the other.

A runner named Cindy experienced her first mile race here and wasn't eager to try another. "Why would you want to do this regularly?" she said after catching her breath, which took awhile. "It's so intense." That's what I've always liked about the mile. It's almost all out, all the way. There's more time to think than in the mad dash of a sprint, but there's none of the marathoner's sense of biding time while waiting for something big to happen. Everything happens quickly in a mile.

Normally the road races I now run are long enough so I don't want to waste any steps in advance, and slow enough so I don't need any. But you can't start a mile cold and expect to warm up along the way, because the race ends two miles before you're hitting your stride. I took care of the preliminaries, then stood around too long and started cold anyway.

The results were predictable. I lumbered and snorted along like a plow horse, with the stride heavy and the breathing loud. The time was my slowest ever in hundreds of mile races. But even a slow mile can have its rewards. This one stretched the bridge to my past into its fifth decade.

FIVE ALIVE

Linda Villarosa, a former editor at *Runner's World*, called me to check a fact about 5K racing. "Didn't you write once that it's now the most popular racing distance?" she said. "How large is it?" I referred her to the head-counters at the Road Running Information Center for the latest numbers, adding that "it wasn't the biggest the last time I checked. The 10K still was, but the 5K was the fastest-growing event."

"Why?" Linda asked, more to make conversation than to collect quotes for her article. She shouldn't have asked "Why?" of someone who overflows with opinions. Two opposite reasons, I told her without mentioning this is also my favorite short race. "This shortest of road distances makes ideal speedwork for the heavy-duty racer, and it's a great place for a new racer to break in."

In support of the first claim I cited Jack Daniels' research findings and coaching success. The exercise-science PhD and coach says the most effective "tempo run" lasts 20 minutes or so—about the time needed to race five kilometers. I held up the Corporate Challenge and Race for the Cure series as evidence of the 5K's drawing power. These events introduce new runners to the sport by the thousands.

Linda Villarosa then excused herself from the phone as the response to her simple question began to sound like a lecture. Left undescribed were other beauties three, four, and five of the 5K:

3. It makes a perfect showcase race for spectators. It can be run on a multilap course (without the lap count becoming confusingly too high) and it can fit nicely into a half-hour TV show (with commercials not cutting into race time).

4. It allows more racing. It's possible to race weekly without pushing the limits of Jack Foster's formula (which calls for one day of recovery for each mile of racing) or the Henderson modification (one day per kilometer).

5. It puts racing within reach of more runners. Those who observe Kenneth Cooper's prescription (of two- and three-mile training runs) feel at home with the 5K distance.

The current 5K racing boomlet doesn't surprise me. I'm more curious about why road racers treated this distance so shabbily for so long. As recently as the mid-1980s, the 5K was cast as an inferior sideshow—a fun run for wimps who were unable or unwilling to compete in the longer main event.

The 5K deserved better. This race has a history as proud as the 10,000's. Both joined the Olympic program in 1912. Three of the sport's legendary figures—Paavo Nurmi, Emil Zatopek, and Lasse Viren—paid equal attention to the two distances. Women got a late start in the five. It didn't become an Olympic event until 1996, but had long established its credibility by then with record-setting by three of the world's top runners: Mary Slaney, Zola Budd, and Ingrid Kristiansen. No one ever called them wimpy.

GEORGE'S DISTANCE

What was once one man's convenient training ground is now a course named in honor of that man. He talked often of running out the door of the hospital where he worked to train on River Road. The man was George Sheehan, who died in 1993. The hospital was Riverview in Red Bank, New Jersey, where he spent much of his medical career. The river was the Navesink, which flows into the Atlantic within view of the hospital. His old training course now hosts the George Sheehan Classic, which moved from nearby Asbury Park and was renamed for him. It was first a 10K and later dropped to his preferred racing distance of five miles.

The ideas that grew into columns, which in turn filled his books, took root on this course. This is also where he developed into a much better runner than most of his readers ever realized. He won hundreds of prizes over a 20-year period beginning in his mid-40s. But some of his best learning came after his cancer arrived, his times slowed, and his winning stopped. He learned here at home how most of his readers, who never stand on any victory platform, feel when they race.

George dreaded the 1987 Asbury Park race, which started within a mile of his oceanfront home. His racing pace had fallen off dramatically since he went on hormone therapy for his cancer. He usually relished the question-answer sessions after his talks. But the night before this race, someone asked a question that stabbed at his heart. "How does it feel to set personal worsts every time you run?" this listener wanted to know.

George's answer: "Embarrassing." He complained that his all-out pace was now slower than he had run the year before in training. He added, "It also can be annoying when people in the trailing edge of a race pack ask me, 'What are you doing back here, Doc?' My first impulse is to say something about, 'What can a runner on drugs for cancer expect?'"

Embarrassment and annoyance didn't keep George from running his hometown race. Afterward he wrote in his weekly newspaper column that his slower pace had taught him an important lesson. "Running back in the pack at Asbury Park was enlightening and inspiring," he said. "I had always written as a representative of the also-rans, but in truth I was always an elite runner—one of the winners. I rarely came home from a race without a trophy, and more often than not was a winner in my age group."

George met runners here who were new to him. He liked what he learned from them. "What I discovered at Asbury Park was that, from leader to last [finisher], the runners were running at the

George Sheehan.

fastest pace they could. The 8-minute milers, for example, were taking no prisoners. They were not—as I once suspected—lollygagging along, engaged in conversation about last night's pasta party. They may not have the maximum oxygen capacity of those averaging two or even three minutes a mile faster, but it was costing them the same effort. They were paying with an equal amount of pain. And for me, gaining ground in this flow was just as difficult as it had been a year or so back at a much faster pace."

George discovered he was not the least bit embarrassed to be seen in the company of these 8-minute milers. Nor would he be later when falling in with 9- and 10-minute crowds. They did what he did: the best they could with what they were given.

15

Training Longer and Shorter

The raceday magic comes at a price. You fly now and pay the fare later. The greater the gap between your normal training and your race effort, the longer is the repayment plan of rest and easy running.

MAGIC MOMENTS

Gordon Hoffert caught me up on the 30-year gap in our friendship at a breakfast in Lewiston, Minnesota. We'd run at the same college in the 1960s but hadn't met since.

"I had my midlife crisis about 10 years ago," said Gordon. "I was teaching and coaching, and trying to decide what I wanted to do next—become a minister or a magician." He chose the ministry but never lost his fondness for magic. At this breakfast, with his son Jess assisting, the Reverend Hoffert made the salt shaker disappear through our table.

"How'd he do that?" I asked Jess. Gordon answered, "Sorry, a magician never reveals his secrets."

Later that day I worked some minor magic of my own. I returned after too long away to play the tricks of the race. The excitement of raceday can double our normal distance range, or it can knock a minute per mile off our everyday pace. I call it "magic" because these improvements seem to appear out of thin air, not as logical conclusions of long training runs or speedwork.

I knew this—and in fact knew the jumps in mileage and drops in time to be conservative estimates. Tripled distances and 2-minute pace bonuses are possible. But I hadn't let races work their magic for awhile. A bad case of PMS (postmarathon syndrome) and a cardiovascular scare had combined to keep me out of all racing for the past six months.

I'd run no short race in more than a year, no timed miles in several months. My daily runs had puttered along slower than ever. I hadn't even planned on racing in Lewiston's Fools Five-Mile. Run in the race, yes, but not race it. I was there to talk afterward and didn't want to fall asleep on stage.

Then an old habit came out of hibernation. That is, to go as fast as possible when running along in a crowd. We won't talk about a time here. By most standards—PR, the last race at this distance, my age-group's leader that day—the time in Lewiston is unworthy of comment. The magic lay in the gap between what my recent slow-motion training logically predicted was possible and what actually happened. My race pace was faster than any other run that year, by almost two minutes a mile.

I'm not revealing any secrets that racers don't already know. Raceday can make magicians of us all.

FLY NOW, PAY LATER

Jeff Galloway enjoyed the best of all combinations for a speaker. He was the one the audience most wanted to hear (because the majority had trained on his program), and he spoke at a time when they most needed to hear him (the weekend of their race). Jeff spoke three times at the Vancouver International Marathon because the room wouldn't hold everyone at once. He asked other writers, including me, to join him up front for the question-answer session.

We heard the usual concerns: What to eat and drink before the race? What to wear during? What to do after? I answered the last one. It's a pet theme of mine because the aftermath is where I've made my biggest mistakes. My favorite catch phrases rolled:

- "The last and least appreciated part of the race begins at the finish line, which is when the all-important recovery begins."

- "You can't run another race until you forget how bad the last one felt, and this can take weeks or months."

- "Expect to suffer from postmarathon syndrome for a month or more afterward. This uninspired feeling protects you against doing too much at the wrong time."

This spiel brought a follow-up question from a man in the audience. "I'm running my first marathon, and my question has to do with the recovery period you're talking about. I don't understand why it would take as much time as you say. I've taken the long runs that Jeff Galloway recommends and don't have any trouble recovering from them. I'm back to normal running in a few days. Why should the marathon be any different?"

If he ran the same way in the marathon that he did while training for it, he wouldn't need any extra recovery time. Then I added, "But you don't train with 2000 of your closest friends. You don't have bands playing or people reading your splits and handing you drinks. You don't have cheering crowds waiting at the end."

When these features of the race come together the result is magical. You can race much farther than you normally train, which is why I can finish marathons on minimal training. Or you can race at a much faster pace than you train for this distance. Jeff

Galloway says we can expect to run two minutes per mile faster in a race than in a long training run of equal distance.

The raceday magic comes at a price. You fly now and pay the fare later. The greater the gap between your normal training and your race effort, the longer is the repayment plan of rest and easy running. For me the formula that now works best is one rest day per hour of the race and then one easy week for each hour raced. Repay now, and I'll fly again later without delay.

Buddy Edelen

Edelen solved the marathon-training puzzle that had generally baffled Americans before him. I paid him this tribute in the April 1997 *Running Commentary*.

As 1962 began, John J. Kelley held the national record at a few seconds above 2:20. He was the last American to win at Boston (in 1957). Leonard "Buddy" Edelen was a young 10,000 runner at the time, not long out of the University of Minnesota. He saw his future in the mara-

© UPI/Corbis-Bettmann

Buddy Edelen (far left).

thon, but not if he stayed in the United States.

Road racing had matured the most in England, so he moved there to race and train. It worked for him. By the end of 1962 he held the

American record at 2:18:57. By 1963 he held the world record at 2:14:28. The price of developing abroad, though, was that he wasn't ever fully appreciated at home.

He never ran Boston because that race paid no travel money then, and his salary as a schoolteacher didn't allow buying plane tickets across the Atlantic. Edelen ran only one marathon in the United States. This was the 1964 Olympic Trial, which didn't make an exception to the qualifying procedure even for a world-record holder.

He ran one of his best races at the Trial in Yonkers, New York—and his most costly. His winning margin on a 90-degree day was 20 minutes. Edelen rushed back into full training five days after the Trial and developed sciatica that limited him to a sixth-place finish at the Tokyo games. A year later his career was all but over because of that lingering injury.

He was only 27 years old when he ran his last fast marathon. This was 1965, when no other American-born runner had yet come within five minutes of Edelen's national record, which lasted until 1969. By then the first hints of a Running Boom were sounding in this country. Heroes of this new era elbowed Edelen aside. He never had a shoe contract, never wrote a book (though a fine one, *A Cold Clear Day*, was belatedly written about him by Frank Murphy), and rarely spoke at clinics. His postcompetitive honors were few.

Buddy Edelen was born a little too soon for all that, and now he has died much too young, of cancer at 59. Remember him, please, for all that he once did—even if you weren't aware of it until now.

NO TRAIN, NO GAIN

My talk to the Portland Marathon Clinic began with a confession of failure. "Two years ago I bragged to this group about trying to perfect the no-training marathon program. I'm back to admit that it doesn't work."

It had almost worked before. I'd finished more than a half-dozen marathons (admittedly slow ones) in the 1990s while barely training. Low training isn't the same as not running. I had run normally (easily but regularly) and yet hadn't done much in the way of special work (long runs). My longest had been half-marathons, and I'd only taken a couple of those. The latest test of low training had been the Royal Victoria Marathon. It hadn't gone well. In fact, it went so badly that I haven't tried another marathon in almost two years.

Warren Finke, one of the Portland Clinic's directors, told his fresh recruits, "Your first goal should be to finish the marathon. Your second should be to look good while you're finishing." I followed Warren on stage and said, "In my last marathon I barely accomplished one of those goals but failed miserably at the other. I somehow finished. But not with style."

Fans along the course often yell, "Looking good." Even when it's not true, they say it. A friend of mine couldn't lie that day in Victoria. He shouted, "You don't look so good. Are you okay?"

I told him, "I look worse than I feel." That was a lie at the moment, but I seemed to recover from the race quickly and returned to normal running—nothing longer than an hour, and a slow one at that—in less than two weeks. But I wasn't nearly out of the hole I'd dug for myself and wasn't ready even for the easy "normals."

The next trip didn't involve racing, just working as announcer at a nighttime event. That morning I ran a standard hour. That midday I partied. And that night I went to work. While onstage I

almost blacked out from a sudden and dramatic wave of dizziness—brought on, I later learned, by some sort of attack on the inner ear (see chapter 8).

Balance was a long time coming back, and I hadn't yet dared run another marathon. But I would someday put the lessons of Victoria to use. Namely, those are "too hard" and "too easy."

"This is my story of failure," I told the Portland marathoners. "But try to see how it might apply to you, and how to keep from making the same mistakes." I could say the same to you readers. See what I did and didn't do, then don't repeat it.

The marathon is challenging, exciting, and memorable, I told this group. But it's also an unnatural act. It's the most difficult act that most runners will ever perform in this sport, and therefore requires the most training. And no matter how well we prepare, the marathon takes a high physical and emotional toll that must be repaid slowly afterward.

PREPAY AND REPAY

I violated both ends of the equation before my last marathon, running too little beforehand and too much, too soon afterward. We'll look at the second mistake first, because it's more common. I've written and spoken dozens (hundreds?) of times about the most important part of the training program being the most ignored. That's the part that starts at the finish line, the part for doing next to nothing, the part that restores balance and keeps you out of trouble.

At the Portland Marathon Clinic I recited the Jack Foster Rule (see chapter 2), one day of recovery for each mile of the marathon, and added my qualifier that "one day per kilometer is even better." I told of the need to run easily—no long runs, no speedwork, and definitely no races—during this four to six weeks. Then I admitted to not following this plan. Oh, I took the required several days off to let the soreness subside.

But then I moved quickly back to normal running, and it was too much when the recovery period had barely begun. Less than two weeks after the marathon, I ran myself into wooziness. I don't say the marathon caused this illness, but inadequate recovery surely set me up for the attack.

Next time I ran a marathon, I would heed this lesson about what not to do afterward. That's to run almost zero the first week, then to take a month or more to ease back up to running easily.

And what to do before? Here's where I had made the too-easy mistake. My pair of half-marathons weren't nearly enough. Maybe if I had run those halves nonstop they might have been barely far enough. I recalled in Portland the Tom Osler adage: "You can instantly double your longest nonstop run by taking walking breaks."

The key word in Osler's formula is nonstop. My longest this way before Victoria hadn't been a half-marathon but a half-hour. Doubling that distance still left me with hours to go. Maybe I could have gone farther by taking more or longer walks. But I didn't. Maybe I could have done better by starting slower. But I didn't.

So it was a long (or should I say l-o-o-o-n-n-ng?) day in Victoria. It turned out that way, predictably, because the practice days hadn't been long enough. "I've learned," I told the Portlanders, "that you can't fake a marathon. If you cheat on the training, the race will eat you up."

Next time I'd do the training right to avoid the raceday bite. This wouldn't mean running higher mileage or extra speedwork or taking fewer days off. No, all I needed were more and longer long runs. By "more" I mean one every three or four weeks for two or three months. "Longer" means going to lengths I'd long preached but seldom practiced in the 1990s—working up to at least three-fourths of projected marathon time instead of settling for half-time work as I'd done before.

"The key to my marathon success or lack of it," I said in Portland, "has always been the length of the longest run. The real running usually ends, and the struggle begins, at about where I leave off in training." Distance doesn't seem to matter much. Time on the road, and on the feet, matters more. If I plan to spend four hours on the road in a marathon, then I need to experience most of that time in training. These longer runs make marathon day seem shorter.

Racing the Long Distances

The risk is that the magic of raceday will overwhelm some runners. This atmosphere leads to adrenaline poisoning, the main symptom being an urge to run too fast, too soon. Resist this temptation.

FILLING THE GREAT GAP

U.S. road racing is running to extremes. The fastest-growing events are the shortest and longest ones we commonly run. At the bottom of our distance range, American 5Ks were booming in the mid-1990s. At the top distance, the number of marathoners stood at historic highs.

Between the extremes, however, growth had leveled off if not stagnated for races in the 8K to 12K range. Distances between 15K and 30K were run the least. This trend was splitting U.S. road racing into two disconnected islands. We had short races and long races, but little in the middle to fill a gap almost 20 miles wide.

I'm a creature of this trend. In the first half of the 1990s, half of my races were 5Ks and half of the others were marathons. A 1995 race showed what I'd missed as an extremist. I ran the Trinity Hospital Hill half-marathon in Kansas City. It's a neatly organized race with a history dating back to the 1970s. Yet it faced the same challenge as other races of its length: how to grow? Hospital Hill's numbers had stayed level for several years.

With almost 2000 entrants it is one of the country's largest halves. But the race is somewhat a victim of its distance. It falls about as far as it can be from either extreme, 5K or marathon. But a bigger problem is a name, half-marathon, that serves the event poorly. No other event takes part of its name from another or comes off sounding like a discounted item. We don't speak of 5Ks as "half-10s." The word *marathon* might frighten away newcomers to the event. And marathoners might think of the "half" as worth only a fraction of the real thing.

The name half-marathon is also misleading. It tempts runners to imagine they can double their time to predict marathon results. Men have broken one hour for the half. But none has come within six minutes of a two-hour marathon. The half-marathon isn't half a marathon in time. It isn't just half as tough to run and doesn't simply require half the training.

The half-marathon is a vastly different race, with its own requirements and rewards. It needs a name of its own. Naming it for a city midway to Athens or Boston won't work. We would still have the connection to full marathons. Maybe race directors could change the distance instead of the name. They might round it down to 20 kilometers (and never start calling it a "double 10K"!).

Name and exact distance aside, the between-the-extremes events are great places to race. Hospital Hill refreshed me on the many attractions:

- Much slower than a 5K, but still fast enough to be a true race and not the survival test that the marathon becomes for many of us.

- Much shorter than a marathon, but still long enough to give the distance workout we might not have taken alone that day.

- Much less crowded than either of the extreme events, which might not please race promoters but is a pleasant escape from the rush-hour traffic of the largest 5Ks and marathons.

PACING THE MARATHON

Steve Meyerson is one of those many people I run across in the course of a year. We talk for a little while at some location far from home, then seldom hear from each other again. E-mail is changing that, though. It's cheaper than long-distance phoning and faster than postal mailing.

Steve has e-mailed me several times from Alexandria, Virginia, since we met at a Jeff Galloway summer camp. Increasingly, his notes centered on the upcoming Marine Corps Marathon. He talked of feeling "sluggish" late in his 20-mile training runs and wondering where he'd find the resources to go the extra 10K on raceday. He then asked, "What pace should I run during the Marine Corps?"

I reminded Steve that race day is magical (see chapter 15). It's worth many extra miles that any runner would find hard to give in a training run. "So don't get overly concerned about running down as you approach 20 miles in the race. This is a whole different experience than training this distance, when you didn't have 18,000 people out there with you, or people giving splits and handing drinks, or people clapping and cheering as you pass."

The risk, of course, is that the magic of raceday will overwhelm some marathoners. This atmosphere leads to adrenaline poisoning, the main symptom being an urge to run too fast, too soon. Resist this temptation, I warned Steve. I've always liked the advice someone (wish I could remember where the credit goes here) gave early in my marathoning life. He said, "Divide it into three parts, and run each one differently."

These aren't necessarily equal thirds. In fact, you hope that the middle one will last much longer than the other two. Treat the first part as the warm-up where you run easily until you clear the early traffic jam (which can be severe in the big-city marathons) and find your running rhythm. This is when you let the early speedsters go, and tell yourself that you'll see many of them later. Do your real running in the second part. This is when you feel strong enough to conquer the world, and it probably will be when you do your best running. In the third part run as well as you can with whatever you have left. This is when the reality of the marathon sets in.

This last part is always tough. It's supposed to be. If it weren't, anyone could do it. But this final part doesn't need to get ugly. If you've paced the first parts right, you shouldn't hit any wall. You should meet again many of the same people who dashed away while you were warming up.

You wish no one a bad day, yet you can't help feeding on these wilting runners. They nourish your sense of momentum as you hold your pace while they've lost theirs. Late in the race it feels far better to be a passer than a passee. Pace the marathon so you can pass people when it means the most.

Oprah Winfrey

Scoff if you want. Joke about the most-reported slow marathon in history. Accuse me of celebrity chasing, in the style of *People* magazine. Writing in the December 1994 *Running Commentary*, I viewed the Oprah Marathon as great news for running. She drew attention to the sport from an audience that doesn't usually notice.

Oprah Winfrey may be a big talker on television, but no one can talk her way through a marathon. She may be one of the most recognized figures in America, but celebrity isn't worth a single mile in a marathon. Oprah turned talk into action. She put in the miles, and she earned the applause of runners for what she did and how she did it.

Understand first that this was no publicity stunt, and that she didn't run the marathon on a whim. If Oprah had wanted maximum exposure, she would have gone to the New York City Marathon. Her publicists would have beaten every media bush in that town. Yet she talked only of running a marathon this fall, without saying where it would be. She popped in unannounced at the Marine Corps race in Washington, D.C.

© Corbis-Bettmann

Oprah's postmarathon comments in the news brought nods of recognition from anyone who has run one. She said, "As I saw the 26-mile sign, I started to cry because I thought, 'Oh God, it's over. It's over!'" Those last two-tenths of a mile seemed to take forever. "Where is it?" she wondered. "Where is the finish?" She finally ran under the clock in 4:29:20, slipping under her $4\frac{1}{2}$-hour goal. One of her first statements: "This is better than winning an Emmy."

Say what you will about Oprah's effort. She did more to introduce our sport to the talk-show-watching, tabloid-reading masses than all the running writers combined. Oprah's fans see her as a friend who comes into their living rooms each afternoon. She gave the marathon a face and a life that most of them had never seen before. She inspired more of these people than all the Olympic gold medalists in history ever could. She may lead some of them away from their TVs and onto the roads.

By running a marathon and putting such a positive spin on it, Oprah becomes our friend, too. We need more runner celebrities like her. Now how could we talk Rush Limbaugh into trying this?

DREAM ON

I'd dreamed of running the Royal Victoria Marathon since first visiting there in another role four years earlier. This is a great race in a gorgeous place. The course is Big Sur without the hills and Napa Valley with an ocean. Three times I promised director Rob Reid to run Victoria "next year." I finally got there, and dreams came true in more ways than one.

After more than 40 marathons, I at last ran one outside U.S. borders. Victoria hardly counts, being one-tenth as far from home as New York City. But I couldn't have picked a better place to go when leaving the country. Victoria lived up to its part of the dream. The race began beside the stately Parliament Building, just above the colorful Inner Harbour and the elegant Empress Hotel.

The weather: perfect at 50 degrees and clearing after heavy overnight rains. The field: up 50 percent from the year before but still comfortably sized at about 2000 runners. After taking a five-mile warm-up loop downtown, we headed out onto the waterfront road that makes up much of the course and is its most attractive feature. That's where the real running began.

Looking back, that's also where I began pushing too hard, too soon. In the late miles another dream of mine came true. It was one of those dreams that often comes the night before a race, and always before a marathon. You know the type: Wake up too late and get to the start after everyone has left . . . can't find your shoes or your race number . . . stumble through a maze-like course up and down staircases inside buildings . . . finish by crawling on your hands and knees.

Those dreams recur. But this one featured new details, and it arose from an incident that really happened. I won't embarrass my traveling companion by giving his full name. We'll just call him Richard. As our trip started, he noticed a tire going flat on his car. "I've owned this Saab since 1983," he said, "and this has never happened before. Maybe it's an omen."

My prerace dream had us needing a ride to the starting line. We found all four of the Saab's tires flat. I told my wife Barbara about the dream. Her instant interpretation: "You're worried about your feet giving out, or maybe just about feeling flat and tired."

I never saw Richard on the course. Later he reported that his feet had failed him. "I had blisters by seven miles and knew it wouldn't

© Ken Lee

be my day. I went halfway, then stopped and walked back here."
His effort wasn't a total loss. He came out of it with a good story.
While making his way to the hotel, a streetwalker of a different sort
approached him (on Broad Street, of all places) and said, "Hey,
good-lookin', would you like some company?" He told her that
unless she could do something for blisters, he wasn't interested.

At about that time my marathon was slo-o-o-wly coming to its
end. I hoped to see Barbara at 25 miles, because I'd rehearsed a
greeting for her. "I'm flat and tired," I would say, "but not retired."
We missed connections, but it's just as well she didn't see me.
Survival shuffling isn't a pretty sight in a loved one.

This time the shuffle looked worse than it felt. My legs refused
to go any faster, but I could still joke with a course monitor, "I'll pay
you to run this last mile for me." He answered with a laugh, "No
way! It's yours to finish." It was, I did, and the memories are better
than the dreams were.

ULTIMATE ULTRAS

Some of my best friends are ultramarathoners. I know them by their attitudes, if not their names, because I once thought the same way. If I couldn't break away from the crowd by running faster, I would do it by running farther. Before the boom of the 1970s you could advertise your differences by racing at any distance. Then the 10Ks grew crowded, so the marathon became your new home. When the number of marathoners climbed until every office and neighborhood had one, runners looking to preserve their uniqueness moved farther out.

Difficulty has escalated, along with distance, as runners must go to greater lengths to escape the conventional running crowd. The need to set trends instead of following them distinguishes the ultramarathoner. Yesterday's marathoners are today's ultrarunners. They are the sport's trailblazers, working the outer boundaries of endurance. They go where few other runners would dare venture, and they have long since left me behind.

As the gap between us has grown, so has my sense of awe over what they accomplish. They not only run very long, but also go very fast for these distances. Yiannis Kouros from Greece averages around $7\frac{1}{2}$ minutes a mile for 24 hours. American Ann Trason runs an even faster pace than that for 100 miles.

Note the focus here on how fast the best ultrarunners go. This suggests that just finishing the distance is no longer enough to gain attention; speed is required. As speed at one distance increases, the escalation to longer distances continues. Events that too closely resemble shorter races and share their record concerns are losing favor with the avant-garde. Once content to use flat roads, they now must cross the Sierras, Rockies, or Appalachians.

The editors of *Ultrarunning* magazine wrote, "One of the clearest trends over the past few years has been the increase in popularity of the trail ultras." They now account for nearly all the largest U.S. races, and size isn't a plus for many of the country's thousands or so ultrarunners. Difficulty has escalated along with distance. One-day ultras in and around cities have grown into multiday races covering whole states (Texas, New York, and Washington in recent years), regions, or countries.

John Loeschhorn, a veteran of mountain racing, graduated to a week-long, 130-mile race through the Sahara Desert. "Each participant was required to be self-sufficient in the desert," wrote Loeschhorn, "carrying all the food, clothing, and supplies needed for seven days. The race organization provided the only water permitted."

With the American continent long since crossed, solo ultrarunners now must run around the United States borders or through each of the states to be different. A Frenchman became the first runner to circle the world. Djamel Balhi reached Paris more than two years and 18,000 miles after starting there. Balhi can go no farther. But his still isn't the ultimate ultra. "I am not a competitor," he said. "I am a traveler."

Count on some racer trying to run the same distance faster, or to make the route longer by passing through more countries.

The problem with escalating distances isn't with the people who run them, but with those who don't. You may think their immense amounts of running devalue yours. You may wonder, "Is this what I must aspire to? Is there something wrong with me if I don't or can't?"

The revolution of the running boom years wiped away the inferiority complex of slower runners and let us be happy with whatever speed we could muster. We learned to admire the fast folks without needing to imitate or envy them. It may be time for another revolution in our thinking. This one would let us take pride in whatever distance we can complete, without feeling diminished by people who do more.

17

Racing at Its Simplest

Every event doesn't have to be huge. There's a place for races of all sizes, just as there is for runners of all speeds. Most races are small, just as most runners are slow. This is both a fact and a strength of the sport.

SMALL TALK

Alvin Chriss, who while working for the Athletics Congress helped ease the sport into its professional era, once claimed that I live in a "wished-for never-never land" of pure sport. He's wrong. In fact, I live in two very different worlds. Alvin and I carried on a friendly battle of words by letter, by phone and, all too seldom, in person. In his work he dealt mainly with fellow running businessmen and politicians.

I am an observer of big-time running. But mostly I still think like a small-time runner, one who wishes that the sport could stay as pure at its high levels as it is for the amateur masses—but knows it can't. During one conversation Alvin complained that I focus too much on "the butterflies of running, the free spirits. You're not what the sport is about now. Your time has passed. Grow with us or be left behind."

I refuse to grow up. Big business and hardball politics may be facts of life at one level of the sport, but very few runners live at that level. They are not what running is about for most of us, or what it means to me most of the time. My job may depend on knowing what goes on at the top. News from there dominates my working hours and written pages, but it occupies few of my thoughts when I run. Nor does the news that the movers and shakers make concern many of the runners I talk with. They care little about boycotts and bans, drugs and blood-doping, prize money and appearance fees, IAAF and IOC rules, sanctions and sponsorship. They don't even memorize results and records other than their own.

I write about these topics and care deeply about some of them. As a running writer and fan, I fit ex-Senator Eugene McCarthy's description of a politician: "Smart enough to know the game and dumb enough to think it's important." But I try not to worry so much about these matters that it infects my running with a misplaced sense of what is most important. I still would rather run a race from the back than watch one from the front. And I still feel that my first duty as a writer isn't to entertain the sport's viewers, but to serve its doers.

They want to know how to go farther, how to go faster, and how to recover from going farther and faster. The doers ask when and where to race. They look first for events that provide the best results (preferably fast times, but at least accurate ones) for a fair price. Then they seek races that offer special excitement.

Any news that doesn't directly concern the doers falls into the realm of trivia and gossip. The big time is of some interest, perhaps, but of no great personal concern to free-spirited "butterflies." They'll continue to live and thrive in never-never land, no matter what happens in the businesslike, politicized world of running that barely touches their own.

IN PRAISE OF SMALL

The woman at the back of the room kept raising her hand, and the panelists up front at the Portland race directors seminar kept recognizing other hand-wavers who sat closer to the stage. Finally, as the program seemed ready to wrap up, this woman shouted her comment. "I hear the other directors talking about how to get their

© Photo Run/Victah Sailer

race numbers up to 10,000," she said. "This is discouraging to our event when we're struggling to draw a field of 300. Why doesn't someone address the role and needs of the small races?" Another race director sitting down front shouted out without raising her hand, "Whatever happened to the saying 'small is beautiful?'"

I was a panelist in Portland that day. My answer began with, "Let me speak up in praise of small races. Let me thank those of you who put them on, because your events are the bedrock of the sport." Every event doesn't have to be huge. There's a place for races of all sizes, just as there is for runners of all speeds. Most races are small, just as most runners are slow. This is both a fact and a strength of the sport. We like to run a megarace once in a while and feel the excitement of strength in numbers. But as a steady diet these events would become overwhelming. We need to balance them by running races that have beauties of their own—those with fields in the dozens or hundreds instead of in the thousands or tens of thousands.

The woman who asked about the place of small races happens to direct one in my hometown. An oddity of Eugene, an acknowledged running capital, is that it has no big road race that pays prize money or draws many runners from out of town. The races are plentiful here, but nearly all are small. Running in Eugene hasn't suffered for not having a big-time race. The races we have here know what their role is, and they play it well. Their job isn't to give a payday to the world's best, isn't to develop Olympians, and isn't to entertain out-of-towners. The first duty of these races is to serve the locals.

Race directors here don't put on expos or carbo dinners, don't bring in guest speakers, and don't produce glossy race booklets. They concentrate on the essentials: a well-measured, marked, and monitored course; adequate drinks; and accurate results. (Okay, they do give T-shirts. Runners wouldn't come out to races of any size without this enticement.) The strength of small races lies in what they don't have: no frills, no high entry fees, no lines or waiting. What they offer is the chance to see other runners as individuals and not just as dots in a crowd.

I told the race directors in Portland, "Some of us old-timers who've been everywhere and seen everything actually prefer the smaller races. The biggies are fun to visit, but the small ones are where we feel most at home."

Y'ALL COME

The summer almost slipped away without my visiting an All-Comers track meet. That would have been my loss. These meets are too much a part of Eugene tradition to miss. They are too much of my history to ignore.

All-Comers are track's version of fun runs on the roads. They're informal events, open to everyone, at little or no cost. They don't offer fancy awards or cheering crowds, but bring athletes out for the simplest and best of reasons. This is a chance to run together for time in an otherwise meetless season.

All-Comers are a Bill Bowerman invention, as far as I can tell. He started them in Eugene in 1949. Bowerman tired of waiting nine months between seasons. He also figured that the seasonal nature of U.S. track was holding the sport down in this country. Runners needed to train year-round, and more meets would give them better reasons to train.

About 40 years ago *Track & Field News* began promoting All-Comers, winter and summer, in the Bay Area and pitched the idea nationally. I got my first taste in Chicago, and it permanently changed my appetite for this sport. This was summer 1960. I'd just turned 17 and was about to start my senior year of high school. Until then I'd been a typical high schooler. I had run only with other boys my age and nothing longer than two miles. The races all seemed serious, even terrifying.

Chicago showed me other sides of the sport: faster and slower, at once more serious and more relaxed. In Chicago I met mature runners. Veterans in their 20s looked old to me then. I even marveled at a few grizzled graybeards in their 30s. Imagine still running at their age! These guys ran longer distances. The two-mile, my previous upper limit, was their sprint. They ran three and six miles at the All-Comers, and led me along with them. I listened in awe to their talk of marathons, and imagined following them there later.

The older guys took their running seriously. Hal Higdon was trying for the Olympic team in the steeplechase. Gar Williams had won national titles on the roads. Yet they betrayed little of the tension I'd always associated with competition. The races were all in a day's work for them. They did their best running between the lines, but could turn off their emotions before the start and after the finish.

153

Higdon and Williams ran faster than anyone I'd ever raced before. They could lap me in a three-mile. But I also saw slower people than I'd ever known before. I could lap Dick King, he of the ragged clothes and shuffling stride. At 40-plus years he was the oldest runner I'd ever seen. King showed me it was okay to grow old and slow and still run races. All-Comers meets would always have room for him.

The All-Comers would always welcome all. That's how they got their name. The meets that Bill Bowerman started in Eugene continue today. I sometimes run here. More often I watch. Here I see myself—past, present, future—in the varied cast of milers. On the track are flashbacks to the young runner whose mile times had started with fours and fives. Here now is the middle-aged runner, with mile times now in the sixes. Here are previews of the old runner, and the seven-minute miles, to come. No one here cheers the fours or hoots the sevens. Everyone is equal, everyone welcome at the All-Comers.

© Ken Lee

Bart Yasso

Races don't come much simpler than the one described in this November 1997 *Running Commentary* article. It ran under the title "Grin and Bare It."

Our busiest traveler at *Runner's World* never writes for the magazine, and doesn't select any articles or art for publication. You seldom see his name in *RW* at all, aside from a tiny listing in the masthead. Yet Bart Yasso comes into direct contact with more runners than anyone else on the staff, and he experiences more adventures than anyone.

At the magazine Bart goes by the title of "race and event promotion manager." This allows him to give assistance to thousands of races each year and to travel to dozens of them. One weekend this fall he dropped in at a race directors' workshop held with the Portland Marathon. There he spoke at a lunch, where the program leader introduced him by promising a humorous program.

It didn't begin with laugh lines, though Bart did treat a pair of serious medical problems lightly. He told of contracting Lyme disease this summer, and how "running hasn't been much fun lately with my joints aching." This didn't stop Bart from making a planned journey to East Africa, to climb Kilimanjaro. While on the mountain he developed paralysis on one side of his face and double vision. He was diagnosed with Bell's palsy, a usually temporary condition often linked to Lyme disease. This wouldn't stop him from making a scheduled trip to a race near Spokane. Bart featured this race in his Portland talk.

It was the Bare Buns Fun Run, a 5K through a nudist camp. Runners have the option of racing with or without clothes. Seventy percent of the 1000 entrants choose to go without, and earn a T-shirt (an odd reward in this case) carrying the coveted designation "Nude." Bart got into the spirit of the day and ran "textile-free." He brought slides to go with his talk, and his audience watched them more intently than would usually be the case at a lecture. One shot showed Bart, wearing only shoes and a big smile while holding a strategically placed number 1.

Bart's plan, despite his illnesses, was "to run my butt off." He displayed a rear view of himself finishing while the clock read "19:95." He said, "It wasn't my fastest time ever. But at least I didn't win the award for shortest in my age group."

SLOW HENRY

"Slow" is in the eye of the beholder. Each of us has times to look down on from whatever peaks we have climbed. Each has a pace below which we won't let ourselves fall—at least not in public. And no place is more public than a track meet. There's nowhere to hide here, as you can in a road race that disappears into the neighborhoods or countrysides.

I'm an old trackman who doesn't run much on the track anymore. When I go to meets, it's usually only to sit and watch. While watching the Hayward Classic masters meet in Eugene, friends who were running asked again and again, "Why aren't you out here?" My answer was always the same: "I'm too old and slow now."

The "old" was a joke. Runners with enough years to be my parents competed here. The "slow" was no joke. I've never been truly fast, and no one else cares that I'm now slow. But I care. Running minutes slower than my old track bests and being lapped repeatedly would have been embarrassing.

So I sat and watched. One runner in particular left me embarrassed about feeling embarrassed. That was Henry Rono. If anyone should shy away from this track meet, it would be Rono. The last person you'd expect to last this long would be Rono.

The same drives that make runners great also prevent them from settling for less than their old level of greatness. You don't see many former record holders competing as masters, because their past comes to haunt them. To them anything less than the fastest time anyone ever ran looks slow.

Rono has one of the sport's greatest pasts. Between 1978 and 1981 he set world records in four events—3000m, 5000m, 10,000m, and steeplechase. Back then he ran some of his finest races at Hayward Field. The best I ever saw was a 1982 win over Alberto Salazar when both came within 10 seconds of the 10K world record.

This past might have haunted Rono. So too might have the sad years that followed: his problems with drinking, his habit of appearing at races (at their expense) out of shape. He stopped showing up as his name lost its sales value. I hadn't heard about him in years, and sometimes wondered how and where he'd ended up.

Suddenly here he was, unannounced in the publicity, at the starting line of a little-known meet for masters. He must have come on his own, because this event paid no fees or expenses. I could have imagined Rono losing himself in a road-race crowd. But this was track, where he had nowhere to hide. He might have run the mile, where the laps are fewer and the comparison with his past isn't as direct. But he chose one of his record distances, the 5000.

Always well rounded from the waist up, Rono was now even more so without looking obese. But from his belt line down, he still looked fit. His stride retained much of its old grace. The old speed was long gone. In Eugene, he ran almost $4\frac{1}{2}$ minutes slower than his 5000 world record. He was almost double-lapped by the winner, whose PR would have left him a lap behind Rono at his best. If this performance shamed him, he hid it well. What he did shamed me for having petty concerns about looking bad.

"I'm getting slower," a friend in his late 60s told me after he ran in this meet. "But if slowing down doesn't bother Henry Rono, I shouldn't let it bother me. The important thing is just to be out here." That's the true spirit of masters running, even on the track where the slowdown is plainest to see. Rono has that spirit. He escapes the shadow of times past and gets out here.

18

Winning Without Beating Anyone

Look back, not just at the people who are running

behind you but especially at those you can't see:

those who don't run and never will . . . those who run

but don't race . . . those who started training for this

race but didn't carry through . . . those who once

raced better than you but no longer run at all. Look at

all the people you've outlasted.

WINNING WAYS

How hard is it to show people how easy it can be to win? It's hardest when you're a parent trying to teach this to your child. I faced this problem when my son Eric was 12 and played team sports for the first time. This was an enlightened program, emphasizing learning over winning. Every kid played in every game, and no one was cut from any team for lack of skill. But scores were kept, and 12-year-olds think they know that winners are those who score the most. Eric's soccer team went the whole season without winning a game and, except for one, without scoring a goal.

"That doesn't matter," I told him. "What matters is that you tried and you improved." He didn't understand. Maybe he never would, so heavy is the opposing propaganda that only the highest-scoring team or highest-finishing athlete gets to feel like a winner.

Young Americans aren't in abysmal shape just because they're lazy, overfed, or too wedded to MTV, Nintendo, and mom's and

© Photo Run/Victah Sailer

dad's taxi service. They're also turned off to sports that adult coaches, sports reporters, and fans have made too hard to win.

My daughter Sarah quit playing organized games after her first try in junior high. Before writing this piece, I asked her why she'd never gone out for high school teams. "They're too competitive," she said. "They cater only to the elite." If you aren't good enough to win, don't bother trying. That's the message kids hear.

What they don't hear is that everyone is good enough to win. And winning isn't everything, it's the only thing—but not in the way that Vince Lombardi meant. Winning on your own terms is the only thing that keeps you going.

Winners never quit, and quitters never win. That's another statement containing more truth than the anonymous author of an inspirational locker-room sign knew. Winning is easier if you take it personally. But that doesn't mean it's without effort or risk-free. No one demands more of you than you do from yourself, but at least in this contest no one can beat you but you.

Thomas Tutko, PhD, a pioneering sports psychologist and author of *Beyond Winning,* calls for redefining the word winner. It has to be more, he says, than, "Did you finish first or didn't you?" In Dr. Tutko's view, the first lesson for runners to learn is that it's less important to finish first than to race the best you can wherever you finish.

"Life is continually competition," said Tutko, "whether you're competing for a job, in school, or in the wilderness trying to survive. There's no way you're going to avoid competition, be-cause it is part of life itself. If we emphasize that it is not competition alone but beating everyone else that is most impor-tant, we've made the burden which is already painful now intol-erable. If we say that losing is like death, then no sane person is going to want to compete." Tutko added, "Maybe the best thing athletics can teach us is not to run away from competition, but to get in there and compete well. This can be a model for not quitting in other areas of life."

WHERE ARE THE AMERICANS?

How you ask the question hints at how you want it answered. If you ask, "What's wrong with U.S. marathoners?" you expect to be told with alarm that they're dropping farther and farther behind the rest of the world, and why. But if you ask, "Is anything wrong with them?" you want to be told with a shrug that nothing is seriously amiss here. Lots of runners asked this both ways after the 1996 Olympics. In Atlanta the first U.S. man finished 28th, the lowest-ranking team leader since 1956. The women did better, but none has had a single-digit finish at the Games since Joan Benoit won in 1984.

Ask me what's wrong here, or if anything is wrong, and I'll answer the same way: "No, nothing serious. Much more is right." Here's why:

• The focus of leading Americans has shifted. The best potential American marathoners aren't running many, if any, marathons—at least not yet. They are sticking with track and cross-country, and possibly laying the groundwork for future marathon success. The shift in focus occurred in the mid-1980s when road running became fully professionalized and there was more money to be made from competing in lots of short races instead of a marathon or two each year. It also occurred because the emphasis in training shifted from quantity (marathon-level mileage) to quality (more suited to 5Ks and 10Ks). And it occurred as marathons came to be seen in this country as big fun runs, hardly worthy of a "serious runner's" efforts.

• Marathoners are aging—and slowing. A generation gap affects U.S. running in general. Track and cross-country are largely young people's sports in this country. Road racing appeals more to the older age groups, particularly the folks who began running for fitness as adults and graduated into low-key racing. Many young athletes see the roads as a place where their parents and grandparents gather. I don't detect any lack of commitment among the young, only some reluctance to mix with the road racers they see as generally uncommitted.

• Training needs haven't changed. The athletes who take the marathon seriously—who still treat it as a race to be won or run as fast as possible—must tune out the fun-run ethic. They must ignore the how-fun-it-all-is stories that fill the running media and return to the time-tested formula: train hard, race hard. The overall trend in marathon training is toward lower mileage and more recovery days, but it can't be that way among the best marathoners. The old Arthur Lydiard formula of 100-plus miles per week still applies to them. The best runners still go at least 20 miles in their long runs.

• Great Americans will rise again. By the 2000 Olympics, America probably will not produce a great wave of marathon stars. After all, the country never has done this before. It was always just one, two, or three at a time. We're overdue for the next one, male or female, but he or she surely will appear when the right people start doing the right marathon training. You can't have a pyramid of runners as wide at the base as it is in the United States without it pushing someone to a high peak.

• The United States leads the world in the statistic that counts most—participation. It's nice to cheer for top finishers from the home team. But it's far greater that we can say, "We have 10 (or 20 or 50) times more marathoners in the United States than any other country has." If the marathon has become a survival test (a term I prefer to "fun run") for most of its runners, fine. These people pay the bills and keep the events healthy.

Jerry Lawson

After Lawson ran 2:09:35 at the 1997 Chicago Marathon—but missed a million-dollar payday offered for the fastest American time ever run—I wrote a letter of praise. His response appeared in the February 1998 *Running Commentary*.

It certainly is nice to see that there indeed are reporters (other than hometown) who believe in me and my accomplishments. I'd known since early in the year that I wanted to run 2:08:30, but it was a very rough year for me runningwise. I was able to run well despite the disengagement from Katrina Price, not because of it. I was totally devastated, missed a few weeks' training and lost about 15 pounds, too. When I started back, I was more worried about the weight than anything. The drawback with being a strength runner and losing that much weight is that a lot of it was muscle tissue, so I had to redevelop the strength I had lost.

I still amazed myself. I ran that time in Chicago from just five weeks of real workouts, with no real base training, and with a shattered heart and head. I also started working two part-time jobs totaling 40 hours a week. One, slightly demanding, is working in a child development center. The other, barely demanding, is working at a running store.

Coach Jack Daniels has done an excellent job of advising me. I believe that had he not been here I would have overtrained and either been exhausted or injured. Jack's workouts and my ability to carry them out better than planned were able to give me enough confidence to chase the million-dollar dream. I was amazed that I ran so well while placing even as much emphasis on the money as I did. I guess I responded to it [the potential payoff] being a time

thing instead of a place thing. I was already chasing times, after all!

As for my goals, I am not focusing on the million dollars. I have found it to be exhausting, both to chase and to answer questions about. I work in two professions where you have to do what you do for the love of it and not for the money. If you're running or working in preschool for the money, you may never get rich monetarily. But the riches you get, and the riches you share, are truly immeasurable.

LAST CHANCE

Talking to runners the night before a marathon, I feel less like a speaker than a psychological counselor. I can't tell them anything about long training runs, which should have ended a couple of weeks earlier, and don't need to psych them up, since the adrenaline in the room is already thick enough to chew. My job is to put these runners at ease, to psych them down.

"Ninety-eight percent of winning," I told the Canadian Rocky Mountain marathoners the night before their race, "is getting to the starting line. You're here. The other 2 percent of winning is getting to the finish line. You're almost guaranteed to do that, so you will win no matter where you finish."

I went on to remind them that we runners make the mistake of only looking ahead and counting how many people are faster on that day. This total can be humbling. "You also need to look back, not just at the people who are running behind you but especially at those you can't see: those who don't run and never will . . . those who run but don't race . . . those who started training for this race but didn't carry through . . . those who once raced better than you but no longer run at all. You're still here. Take pride in wherever you finish. Look at all the people you've outlasted."

Those last words would revisit me the next morning. I wouldn't finish the Rockies Marathon; I never planned to go that far. But I did want to start with the marathoners and put in some good training for the next full one. The race began at the Nordic Centre in Canmore, Alberta. Site of cross-country skiing at the 1988 Winter Olympics, it sits 500 vertical feet above the town. We ran downhill for the first two miles. Or rather, I tiptoed to protect cold and creaky legs from damage from this jarring wake-up call.

A mile or so into the event I heard the voices of three men behind me. That's normal. Marathoners talk a lot in the early miles. The abnormality this time was that I heard no footsteps. Usually there would be a pitter-pat of feet on the road, especially as they brake on a slope like this.

Finally I turned around. Mystery solved. These weren't runners but bicyclists. "We're riding sweep," one of them told me. They followed the final runner, and I was it. I'd never run last before, even briefly. Oh, it happened on the track but never on the roads. I thought the race directors hired someone to run last so no one would feel embarrassed.

Looking back, I saw nothing but an empty road behind the bicyclists. This position didn't embarrass me. Last is not least. The last runner still leads everyone who isn't there.

LAST SUPPER

You don't get many chances to have first experiences, especially not at my age. But I had two firsts in as many years at Canmore, Alberta. One was starting in last place at the 1996 Canadian

Rockies Marathon. This experience provided the theme for my talk here the next year.

I spoke again at the marathon's prerace dinner. George Sheehan called such meals "last suppers." He said we attend them more for the communion than for the carbos. The term last supper never fit better than here. For the first time I spoke in a church, St. Michael's Anglican. This almost inspired me to say something Sheehanesque. But I'm less steeped in religion than George was and couldn't think of any lines from him to parrot. The church looked out on the race finish line, so I pointed to it as "tomorrow's promised land."

I've yet to experience finishing last in any race. My best is still better than that. But that word "last" has become a favorite of mine. My main goal in running is to last—to finish as late as possible in this race of a lifetime. "Winning," to borrow one of George Sheehan's best lines, "is never having to say I quit."

PART III

Best Years

19

Gaining Much From Little

We average runners are still exceptional human beings, at least in terms of our ability to move far and fast on foot. We might only make the 50th percentile among runners but rank in the 99th among all people. We don't need to run very far or fast to stand out from that crowd.

SHORT STORY

It could have been an awkward moment. I knew him only as a voice on the phone and a name on a notepad. Now we were to meet in a crowded cafe. How would we spot each other? Not a problem, as it turned out. He saw me enter, stood, and said, "I recognized you from the picture in *Runner's World.*"

After sitting down, he added, "I have to admit to being a little surprised. I'd expected someone much taller." I hear this a lot. Being thought of as something I'm not is more amusing than annoying. The standard answer: "Yeah, that postage-stamp-size picture does make me look bigger than life." Still, this is an odd way to open a conversation. It's like saying, "From your phone voice I expected someone much better looking." Or, "From your picture I thought you would have better things to say."

Despite what the *RW* photo shows of my head and shoulders, I'm short. I never grew taller than 5 feet $5\frac{1}{2}$ inches, and probably have lost that half inch. Another standard line, usually delivered at talks: "I used to be 6 feet tall, but all this running has pounded me down to what you see now. You hear about losing weight by running, but no one has told you about losing height."

My mom passed down her size, and blessed me with an attitude about it. She topped out at 4 feet 10 inches, and her brothers at 5-2 and 5-4. At a wedding, someone from the other family was heard to say about us, "What is this, a convention of short people?" But I never thought of the King family as tiny. They had big personalities, and they never let short mean insignificant.

Being short doesn't hinder me much. I can't reach a top shelf without a stepladder, and my neck sometimes aches from looking up into faces all day. Otherwise lack of size is no handicap. It has advantages:

- You take up less space in a crowded world.

- You block no one's view at movies or parades.

- You never have to duck through doorways.

- You can always sit in an airplane seat or a compact car without cramping up.

- You don't look down on anyone older than 13.

- You don't have the opposite sex pestering you for your body.

- Your physical presence threatens no one.

- You aren't asked to do much heavy lifting.

- You can buy pants in kid sizes, which are cheaper.

- You can eat less food because your size gives you fuel efficiency.

Mostly, though, you have a perfect sport. As a kid I was too short for my first love, basketball, and too small (and scared) for football. But running didn't reward the tall or penalize the small. Back then I could look most runners in their eyes without tilting my head backward. They were fellow refugees from sports that favor bulk.

Runners now come in all sizes. But it still has a special place for compact bodies, built for flight. In races we can tuck in behind the oversized people and let them break the wind for us. Then we can pick up one of the smaller T-shirts that run out last. As long as both feet reach the ground, we're tall enough.

© Photo Run/Victah Sailer

ONCE AN ATHLETE

The hardest insults to swallow are the ones that are true. Which explains why I take such offense when told, "Runners aren't really athletes." Oh yes, we have endurance—some would call it a high tolerance for boredom. Our legs look like they were chiseled from granite. We look athletic, at least from the waist down. We're slim. Our hearts thud along slowly. Most of us have arteries the size of water hoses.

But if athletes are defined by their quickness, agility, strength, and hand-eye coordination, few runners qualify. Our skill is quite specialized. We're good at putting our feet down endlessly, and that's about all.

I wasn't a bad athlete as a kid. If granted more size, I might have been a good one. But my running had nothing to do with this. I was more athletic before starting to run than after. Whatever talent I showed then was the result of practicing those specialties— summer swimming, football in the fall, basketball all winter. Once that practice ended, the skills eroded.

Back when I could barely run a full mile, I'd swim that far just for fun. Today I could run a mile in my sleep but couldn't go two lengths of an indoor pool without feeling like I'd sprinted a mile in combat boots. As a kid I could pass a football one-third the length of a field or catch one thrown just as far. Now I couldn't toss a ball 10 yards or gather one in from 10 feet away. Once, I could graze the basketball rim with my fingertips (which is no mean feat for someone who never reached $5\frac{1}{2}$ feet of height). These days my vertical jump wouldn't let me leap over a sleeping dog. I couldn't reach the bottom of the basketball net without a stepladder.

These old skills are long gone. Others never fully developed. I once dabbled in ice skating on the frozen waters of Iowa. The last time I skated, the outing ended with a splat on the rink and a couple of cracked ribs. Now I live in a cross-country skiing paradise. The Cascades are only an hour away, and their snow is reliably deep from November to April. My future wife Barbara lured me to a mountaintop our first winter together, where a tumble in this supposedly safe sport dislocated my shoulder. That trip cured me of cross-country skiing. Or so I thought.

Then my son Eric acquired a passion for snowboarding. One winter he talked me into going with him to the mountains. I

wouldn't mount a snowboard, heaven forbid, or ever strap on downhill skis. Even looking up at the lifts terrifies me. I only agreed to try cross-country again after a seven-year recovery from the last attempt. I managed to stay upright most of the time on the flats and uphills. But downhill . . . this would have been hilarious if it hadn't happened to me. I'd forgotten that skis don't come with brakes and a steering wheel. On the slightest downgrades I careened out of control. After a few awkward dives and splats, I took off the skis and walked back to the parking lot.

Before the winter's snows melted, I returned for another try. Only this time it wasn't on skis but in snowshoes. Snowshoes grip the snow instead of slipping across it. Anyone who can walk can cover ground the first time out without falling. Walking I can do. It requires minimal athletic talent, which is all this runner has and which is why I took an instant liking to snowshoeing.

Phyllis Gallant

This chapter talks about getting much from little, but Phyllis did even more. She gained something from nothing—no training, that is. Here's her story from the June 1996 *Running Commentary*.

My talks to marathoners advise, "One of the attractions of your event is that it takes months of preparation. You can't just wake up one morning and decide to run a marathon that day." Most can't, or won't, or shouldn't. But Phyllis Gallant could, and did.

We met at the Okanagan International Marathon in Kelowna, British Columbia. Her husband, Vince, had brought her there from Edmonton to hold his sweats and whatever else nonrunning spouses do while waiting for their mates to pass their hours on the road.

The three of us ate lunch together the day before the marathon. Phyllis, a mother of three, said she didn't run but walked for exercise. Sometime that afternoon she fell under the spell of Nick Lees. He's an Edmonton legend—a British-born newspaper writer also known as Nick Danger. "He indulges in such ventures as climbing mountains and jumping out of airplanes—all without any special preparation. He also runs marathons—without admitting to training for them, of course. He enlisted companions at Kelowna to run with his Back of the Pack Gang. Not finding enough volunteers, he turned to Phyllis and challenged her with, "I bet you couldn't finish a marathon"—saying it the British way, "mahr-thun."

She took the bait. Then she did another no-no: bought a new pair of shoes to use for the first time in this event. Darned if she didn't win the bet by finishing. It took something over five hours, but she made it.

The next week Phyllis signed up for the Learn to Run Class at a Running Room store. At least she hadn't already realized that she didn't want to run any more, as some people do after rushing into a marathon too quickly and with too little preparation. Phyllis came back to Kelowna this spring to celebrate the first anniversary of her marathon debut. This time she had trained during Edmonton's cold (the locals say, "We have 10 months of winter and 2 months of bad skiing") to make another run at the distance. She took an hour off last year's time, then vowed, "Now I'm going to join the Running Room's Marathon Training Clinic."

LAW OF AVERAGES

I've spent much of my running life practicing abnormality. I ran to be different, not just from people who didn't run but from other runners as well. Early on I ran to be noticed. At my size I couldn't stand above the crowd, so I'd stand apart from it.

When other kids in high school played football and basketball, I ran. When they trained for track only in the proper season, I ran year-round. When other runners ran short, I went long. When they raced on the track, I took to the roads. When they ran five-mile races, I tried marathons. When they progressed to marathons, I moved to ultras. When their training was short and fast, mine was long and slow. When they started running long steadily, I began taking walking breaks.

For a long time I liked feeling abnormal. Only in my middle years did I recognize my "differences" were more imagined than real. I am, and probably always have been, unremarkably middle-of-the-road. I grew up in the middle of the country and in the middle of the century. I'm moderate in both my political views and personal habits. My income roots me firmly in the middle class, meaning someone who earns too much to go on welfare and too little to pay all the bills.

As a runner I'm also middle class. That is, I run more than needed just to stay fit but less than required to make any racing waves. My mileage would make an exerciser wince and a competitor laugh. After going to the extremes of short track races and then road ultras, I settled back to the middle distances. My favorite events now fall into the gap between 10K and marathon.

I started at the back of the pack, rose briefly to the top in small-time competition, but soon eased back into my proper place. I'm much slower now, but so is the sport. I still finish almost precisely in the middle. My biggest race ever was a New York City Marathon in which 29,000 of us finished. My place: 14,500th.

So I'm truly Joe Average. Come to think of it, that isn't a bad way to be. We average runners are still exceptional human beings, at least in terms of our ability to move far and fast on foot. We might only make the 50th percentile among runners but rank in the 99th among all people. We don't need to run very far or fast to stand out from that crowd. Being abnormal by its standards is enough of a distinction without also trying to separate ourselves from other runners.

Scanning my best memories as a runner, I find few that were solo. The standouts: team training and relay racing as a kid, and long group runs and group travel to races as an adult. All involved running with others, not against or away from them.

No less an observer than George Sheehan, once a self-described loner, wrote in his late years, "Where there were once too many people in my life, now there are too few." He joined a running group. "Now I look forward to running with people," he noted in his last book, *Going the Distance*. "I need people to talk to, I need people to listen to, I need people to be with." Running became George's team sport. "I now have comrades," he said. "I am a member of a gang."

Somewhere in my middle years, maybe while working on the Sheehan biography *Did I Win?*, I realized that being a loner was lonely. I needed to run more with people most like myself, to quit flaunting my few differences from them, and to start sharing the many likenesses of our gang.

TOUGH ENOUGH

The book was titled *Think Fast*. Its original subject was mental toughness training for runners who race, and only toughness. I talked the publisher, Stephen Greene Press, into an equal emphasis on smartness. Two reasons: (1) Too many tough runners drive themselves out of the sport because they aren't smart enough to control their toughness, and (2) too many smart runners drop out because they aren't tough enough to exercise their smartness. You need both the mental muscle and the wisdom to use it.

You may not think toughness is a trait of yours. But all runners who race have a certain amount of toughness, and with training can become even tougher. Running toughness isn't like the meanness an NFL linebacker directs against an opponent. Ours is a quiet, long-suffering toughness—a survival instinct rather than a killer instinct—directed as much inward as outward.

In distance racers' terms, toughness means starting and finishing, enduring and improving, weathering problems and correcting mistakes. Toughness means knowing when to push on and when to pull back, when to psych up and when to calm down, how to be single-minded and to fit running into a full life. Your toughness is made up of equal parts persistence and experience. You don't so much outrun opponents as outlast and outsmart them, and the toughest opponent of all is the one inside your head.

Two pioneering sports psychologists, Bruce Ogilvie, PhD, and Thomas Tutko, PhD, exposed the runner inside me who appears to be rather wimpy. Late in my serious-racing career (too late to do me much good there) but early in my writing life (soon enough, I hope, to do some readers some good), I took their test of 11 desirable traits in competitors. It ranked me against the thousands of athletes tested at Ogilvie's and Tutko's Institute for the Study of Athletic Motivation. Higher scores on the 100-point scale meant greater mental strength, and vice versa. Three of my traits vied for last place, none with better than a 15th-percentile rating: leadership, aggressiveness, and mental toughness.

Ogilvie and Tutko didn't use the word *wimp* to describe me. Instead, they called me *tender-minded.* I accept either term as accurate. I've never trained even one of the 100-mile weeks that are standard practice for harder-working runners. I've never once collapsed from exhaustion as stronger-willed athletes do when they push too far. But I've still done pretty well as a runner—winning some state high school titles and a college scholarship, and later playing a small role in some of the nation's biggest events.

Distance races aren't so much runner-against-runner competitions as runner-against-self. Testing one's own outer boundaries can be thrilling but also painful. Some training runs are harder than others. But none is truly easy. Because running offers no version of a walker's stroll, a swimmer's float, or a biker's coast, it can more quickly wear you down.

My running in all or parts of five decades and racing hundreds of times shows a form of toughness. I've been tough enough to survive. If my limited mental muscle has carried me this far, then you too surely have enough to succeed. You may just need two compensating strengths.

1. If you can't be a fighter, then be a lover. Learn to love running so you'll want to keep doing it, and by doing more will grow fitter and faster without fighting yourself or anyone else any harder.

2. If you can't get tougher, then get smarter. Learn tricks for getting the most success from your available raw material of body and mind.

20

Living Out the Legacy

"Make the most of life. Live it intensely because it will pass all too fast. For too many people life is what happens when they're planning something else."

—Paul Reese, oldest trans-American runner

DAYS OF OLD

My readers (and I sometimes forget that a few of you are out there) not only know me mostly by my postage-stamp size picture that runs with my column in *Runner's World* and think I should be taller, they also think I should be faster. I recall the first time a reader saw me lingering in my accustomed midpack position and shouted, "If you're so smart, what are you doing way back here?"

Here's a new twist to this old theme. It shows how far I've traveled from the days when the *RW* column didn't carry a picture and readers might say, "I expected someone older." I never hear that anymore. I've aged into my job that readers expect to be occupied by a graybeard. Now I'm the expected age—at least.

One early morning I stopped at Kinko's on the way to a run. Understand that I do no grooming before running. Face is unshaven, hair unbrushed, eyes still puffy from sleep. The 25-ish clerk looked me over as I walked to the cash register. Then he asked, "Are you the same one who writes for *Runner's World*?"

Yes, I said, smiling at being recognized. This rarely happens in my hometown. The smile froze and then drooped as the young man announced, "You're old!" Then he added, "You're older than your picture in the magazine. It needs updating."

I told him that shot, taken by my wife Barbara, was only a year old. "Well, you've aged since then," the clerk said. Recovering slightly, I told him, "I have been on this earth for a long time, and I've written for the magazine for 30 years."

That's longer than this kid has been alive. "You must be a runner to know me," I said. Now he smiled for the first time. "Sure am. I'm going out for a run in . . . " He looked at his watch. "Twenty minutes when I get off work."

"Nice to meet you, uh . . . " I looked at his nametag. "Scott." I told the story to Barbara, who was waiting in the car. We both laughed. But this episode kept gnawing at me until I finally had to write it down. This Kinko's kid had struck a nerve. Did I really look so old? Has my aging accelerated? And why should this bother me?

I had thought a lot about age lately, and for good reason. My father never got his chance to be elderly, or even to spend enough time in middle age. He died shortly before his 55th birthday, which seemed younger to me all the time. I would soon become older than Dad was allowed to be, and realized it's better to look old than never to get the chance.

FATHERS' DAYS

Looking over my left shoulder as I write are two photos. One pictures my father, the other a man I've often called a "second father." The first photo shows my real dad, sitting with his three brothers at the Drake Relays in Des Moines. He was younger then than I am now. He would die—much too young but not before passing his passion for the sport on to me—within a year after this shot was taken. The other photo now watching over me in the office has George Sheehan greeting runners at a Tyler, Texas, race finish line in the last year of his life. George was my running-writing confidant for his last 25 years.

He was the real father of George Sheehan III. We took the stage in Edmonton, Alberta, to talk about Dr. George's legacy. He handed it down most directly and strikingly to his eldest son (one of the 12 Sheehan children). The dad was smaller and more wiry, but young George—his longtime business manager—carries on the sound of his father's voice, the Irish gift for storytelling and the ease onstage.

Young George was now about the same age that his dad was when he started writing for *Runner's World* in 1970. I saw unmistakable reflections of him then in his son now. And I saw more and more of my own father in my aging self. He was taller and darker, but the family resemblance deepens with each new line in my forehead, gully in the cheeks, and sag under the chin.

After the Sheehan show in Edmonton I traveled to Flint, Michigan, for my once-a-year stint as a TV commentator. This forced me to watch myself during the editing of this program. The effect was startling. Here on the screen, on what would have been Dad's 80th birthday weekend, I saw his mannerisms in my own: the tight smile and nervous flutter of the hands while conversing with strangers, the slight stutter and wince when searching for the right words under pressure.

Of course, it was Dad who put me on the course that led to Edmonton and Flint. From him I inherited running and writing. He was an athlete while young and a fan of track for life. He wrote for newspapers and magazines in the first of his several careers.

He taught me that this is an exciting sport and a noble profession. I've been lucky enough to combine the two for most of my lifetime. I fell for his twin loves early and have never doubted that they are right for me. He didn't just point the way and turn me loose. I see more clearly with each new birthday that he's still here with me. He has shared this wonderful journey every step and word of the way—not just by looking down from a nearby photo or from afar, but by looking out from inside.

AGING WELL

Two of my favorite people turned 80 within a month of each other. My mother celebrated quietly, insisting, "I don't want any party." Paul Reese kept celebrating the rest of the year.

Mom reached 80 in good shape after beating back two rounds of colon cancer. Arthritic knees had slowed her stride, but she was vigorous in every other way. This included writing a weekly newsletter to circulate within our family and to her friends. She never missed a week. Nor did she miss many basketball games or track meets at Drake University, from which she graduated in her 50s after putting three of her kids through school there. She celebrated her birthday early every year, without labeling it as such, at the Drake Relays.

Paul Reese's wife Elaine overruled his protests and organized a party of 100 for his 80th birthday. I couldn't be in the Sacramento area with them, but it's just as well. I would have come away well roasted. Paul has a gently biting sense of humor, and he'd planned to refer to me as "a bow legged pig farmer from Iowa who habitually slithers past me in the last few miles of a race."

My present to him was the edited manuscript for his book, *Go East Old Man*. This is a sequel to *Ten Million Steps*, his report of a run across the United States at age 73 (see chapter 6). Paul wrote in the second book about running across all the remaining states west of the Mississippi River except Alaska and Hawaii. He would get to those later. Again he kept a daily diary of the travels, and again I had to squeeze out half of his original text to reduce the material to book size. He says, "If you had come to the birthday party, you would have cut my 15-minute talk to $7\frac{1}{2}$."

He asked at the end of the *East* book: "Where do we go from here? Well, at vintage 80, my first priority is to stay alive. And along those lines I must admit to being somewhat surprised and immensely pleased with my continued existence. As to where we are running, the battle plan Elaine and I have is to try to (no guarantees here!) cross the remaining 22 states. Barring any disasters to Elaine, me, or the motor home, we think the time will come when we will be able to say we have run across all 50 states. If that does happen, you can bet that we will be telling all about it in another book."

After the party Paul and Elaine (plus their two Labs, Brudder and Rebel) departed on a quest to complete the other states—which they did before Paul turned 81. No one older has run across the United States I don't know of anyone, at any age, who has crossed every state this way.

In his birthday talk Paul shared his advice for aging so well. It also applied to my mother at 80: "Make the most of life. Live it intensely because it will pass all too fast. For too many people life is what happens when they're planning something else." He then borrowed a line from a much-younger man, singer Jimmy Buffett: "I'd rather die when living than live when I'm dead."

Johnny Kelley

No one has lived more marathon history than Kelley. I wrote about his legacy in the September 1996 *Running Commentary.*

Johnny Kelley was a blue-collar marathoner, as most runners were before the sport turned up-scale in the 1960s. He served out his working years with the local electric utility, Boston Edison. Kelley never graduated from college, but recently Boston University made him an honorary Doctor of Humane Letters. Too

© UPI/Corbis-Bettmann

bad the sport doesn't have some way of honoring him with a "doctor of marathoning" degree.

The Boston Marathon is only 10 years older than he is. As a child he watched the marathoners there. Later he won the race twice and finished near the front on many other occasions. As the years piled up, his speed backed down, but he continued to run the marathon each spring until the age of 84, when his 61st Boston was his last.

Having seen so much of marathon history, Kelley would say that the most exciting time to be a marathoner might be now. Never have so many people of such widely ranging abilities run this event. Sixty times more runners entered Boston in 1996 than came there in 1967,when my path first crossed Kelley's.

He had already helped change the direction of my running. I'd run out of improvement on the track and was looking toward the longer distances. I'd heard about Kelley long before seeing him. I'd thought that if an old guy like this (almost 60 at the time) can still run marathons, what's stopping me from running one at my age (only 23)? He would slip out of the top 100 finishers that day. The 1967 Boston would be his last run under three hours.

Somewhere around the halfway point in Wellesley I passed Kelley. He didn't look my way or hear my shout of good wishes. I was just another runner among the tens of thousands who passed through his years at Boston. Mine was just one among the millions of voices that rained down on him from one end of the course to the other. The honors flowed two ways for anyone who crossed paths with Johnny Kelley at Boston. We honored him for all he had done and continued to do, and we felt honored to be on the same course with someone who had lived so much marathon history.

FOUNDING FATHER

News of Bert Nelson's death took two days to travel the 500 miles up to Oregon from Mountain View, California. It arrived as a two-inch item in the morning newspaper, a small and sad way to hear about the passing of a giant in my life. Bert cofounded *Track & Field News* with his brother Cordner shortly after World War II. It was the first of the modern magazines on this sport and still might be the most respected. Both brothers are members of the National Track and Field Hall of Fame.

Bert edited *T&FN* for nearly 40 years, yielding that post only as his Parkinson's disease would no longer let him do the job he expected of himself. He died at 72. I remember him as 42. That was his age the summer I first walked into his office as an awestruck kid spending a summer bumming around the San Francisco area running circuit.

T&FN had fed my dreams through high school and into college. I was now a pilgrim, going to the source. That was a cramped storefront in Los Altos, but it looked like Mecca to me. Bert Nelson dressed casually and rode an ancient bicycle to work (in an era when executives did neither), but he struck me as regal.

Bert let himself be bothered by a nobody from nowhere. I had no ambitions to make journalism—let alone running journalism—a career. I just thought it would be neat to spend a summer at Mecca, and pestered Bert's staff until odd jobs opened up for me. One of them was mowing Bert's and Jeanette's yard. I felt honored to do it.

If we're lucky, we find one person in a lifetime who changes our life's course. Bert Nelson was that person for me. Seeing the good life he'd made for himself convinced me to bail out of teacher-coach training and take journalism classes. He plucked me off my first full-time job, with a newspaper, to return to *T&FN*. He published my first book. Of all the people I've met in 30-plus years of writing work, none has left a greater impression than Bert Nelson. When naming role models, I can't think of a better one than the first one.

Bert could have succeeded in almost any field. He had the smarts and skills for teaching, along with a keen business sense. He could have edited, written for, or published much more lucrative journals than *T&FN*. But this was his baby, his family, his home. He was content there. He stayed there for almost 50 years.

Bert wasn't much of a runner. He competed in high school and one year of college, then stopped. But he had the trait that we runners admire most: endurance, which can take many forms besides athletic. His good works endure even now.

The day that news of his death reached Eugene, I wanted to share these thoughts right away with his staff, widow, and daughter. But first I had another column to write, then a journalism class to teach, then a book chapter to polish. This took most of the day.

"With all that work finished," I wrote in the letter, "it now occurs to me that it's the best possible tribute to Bert. None of it—not one bit—would have been possible without his early help. He helped put us all where we are now. We feel sadness today. But we also feel enormously proud to be part of his living legacy."

21

Reading, Writing, and Running

Reading about the stars of the sport can be intimidating. You can feel pangs of inferiority on learning
about athletes who train more in a day that you do all
week . . . or run more to warm up than you do in
your whole workout . . . or go two miles for each one
of yours when they race. The cure for intimidation
isn't to stop reading. It's knowing how to read.

NEWS FREAKS

Not all runners enjoy reading about the stars of the sport. Some find this news too disturbing. At my most impressionable age, I devoured *Track & Field News*, *Long Distance Log*, and anything else written about the sport. My young teammates didn't share this passion. Instead they told me of choosing not to read what happened at the highest reaches of the sport. The news of better runners depressed them. They felt it diminished their own efforts.

My buddies didn't know how to read these magazines. They didn't understand the true nature of news stories. I knew from growing up in a family of journalists and studying to become one myself. Journalists-to-be learn a truism of this business in their first course. "If a dog bites a man," the saying goes, "that's not worth reporting. But if a man bites a dog, that's news."

Normal people and events aren't newsworthy; only the oddities are. News tells of the exceptions, not the rules. Sports lend themselves to this type of reporting, because standouts are so easy to see and dote upon. Sports worship their winners, and spread the notion that only one athlete or team can win any event, and give the impression that to win anything you must win everything—the Super Bowl, the Final Four, the Olympic gold.

Sports news tells recreational athletes that we must think, and train, and compete like those who make the headlines. But they're not like us. This is their job. They play for pay and plan their day around this work, while we try to squeeze our sport around the edges of the workday. They chose their parents well. They have the size and skill, speed and stamina to compete with the best athletes in their sport, while we lack the gifts to win anything more than a local award when only three people show up in our age group. They are freaks. Unpleasant meanings of that word aside, they're one-in-thousands athletes who climb to the peak of their sport, while we form the base of the pyramid on which they stand.

Running doesn't suffer as badly from worship-the-winner syndrome as most sports. We generally take a healthy everyone-can-win approach. Yet the running media still honor the man-bites-dog definition of news by focusing on who's up top. Reading about them can be intimidating. You can feel pangs of inferiority on learning about athletes who train more in a day that you do all week . . . or run more to warm up than you do in your whole workout . . . or go two miles for each one of yours when they race.

The cure for intimidation isn't to stop reading. It's to know how to read. Realize that these people have been written up because they are exceptional. Admire the "freaks." Take inspiration from them. But don't let their uncommon efforts insult your common ones. Know that you are among the 99 percent of readers who are normal.

Take pride in your training, knowing that megamileage runners can't log one of your miles for you. Celebrate your racing, knowing that record-setting runners can't break any of your PRs. Once you start thinking this way, the news stops disturbing you. The "freaks" of running can only lift you up, never put you down.

Bob Anderson

His is a name you don't hear much anymore. You never see it in the magazine he founded, yet everyone who works there now owes him a debt, as does the whole sport. This story on Anderson ran in the August 1996 *Running Commentary*.

Thirty years ago as a high school boy in Kansas, Anderson wanted to read more about his favorite sport, so he started a magazine, *Distance Running News*. It took so much of his time and attention that he dropped out of college.

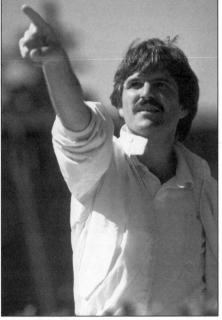

© Ken Lee

Later he moved to California and changed the magazine's name to *Runner's World*.

I joined him then as his first editor. We stayed together, in several capacities and various degrees of peace, for most of the next 15 years. In 1985 he sold the magazine to Rodale Press and apparently dropped out of the sport. Since then I haven't seen or talked with Bob Anderson, but I've often wondered how he is doing since leaving running publishing.

As the oldest and biggest of the sport's magazines marks its 30th birthday, you might also wonder about its founder. Mark Winitz answers this in *The California Schedule* magazine.

Now 48, Bob manufactures and markets women's swimsuits from *RW's* old hometown of Mountain View, California. He runs as he never did while owning the running magazine. "When I was involved in the business of *RW*, I never had the time to train," he tells Winitz. His usual week was a Sunday race and nothing else.

"Now I have a lot more time for my own running," he says. "I haven't missed a day of running in over three years." He recently broke 36 minutes for 10K and is approaching 17 minutes for 5K.

Only when he talks about racing does Bob's old hard edge show. The competitive juices that he once funneled into the running business now go into his races. "I think jogging is boring," he says. "If I were a jogger, I wouldn't bother with the activity at all. To me running has always been a sport rather than just recreation. That's why I was always willing to promote anything that got people into racing."

Bob Anderson promoted well. His magazine gave the developing sport its first and longest-lasting national voice, for which we can thank him. He gave me a career, for which I thank him.

TESTING POSITIVE

Stories like this don't usually come with happy endings. This one still might not, but it certainly sounds good so far. The news reached me in a newspaper article from the St. Paul *Pioneer Press*. Bruce Brothers wrote about Mike Seaman, who led all masters in the local Human Race 8K. He ran 26:39. That time for a 44-year-old could stand on its own merits, without qualifying details. But those details make Mike Seaman's story remarkable.

Runner's World had profiled him several years earlier. Writer John Brant told of Seaman testing positive for malignant melanoma at age 32. There is a dismal survival rate for this type of skin cancer. Seaman underwent the usual aggressive treatments, which pushed the disease into remission. Then, seven years after his original diagnosis, the cancer attacked again.

By this time his marriage was failing along with his health. He rejected the slash-burn-poison therapies of surgery, radiation, and chemo, and just left town, moving from his home state of Minnesota to the West Coast. He was either looking for a new way to live or a nice place to die. At the time he didn't know which it would be. When Brant visited him in 1991, Seaman was living on California's Monterey Peninsula. True to his name, he had gone to the sea to work as a kayaking guide. He appeared to be well, and well adjusted to whatever turn his medical condition might take next.

I'd heard nothing more about Seaman since the *RW* story ran. I wasn't even sure that he had survived for another four years until Bruce Brothers' story arrived. He reported that Seaman was still healthy and just getting back into racing. Mike attributed his recovery partly to nutrition but largely to "imagery, visualization, attitude change." He could give testimonials to the power of positive living, which he has practiced since moving to California in the late 1980s.

"I created my own environment by eliminating television, radio, and negative people," he told reporter Brothers. "You turn on the news, and what's the first thing you hear? Murder. The second thing, war. Sometimes now I'll turn on the radio, hear that stuff, laugh, and flick it off. I don't have a TV. I don't have a stereo. I don't need to listen to those love-gone-wrong songs. That tears me up."

Seaman figured his body already was trying to tear itself up from the inside. He didn't need to deal with forces tearing at him from the outside, so he got rid of the negatives he could control. He had run away from home, then realized a few years ago that his fight was too lonely. He needed help with it, and wanted to give help to others. After rejoining his family and friends in Minnesota, the one-time running-store owner launched a pair of new careers, both of which involve helping people. He went to work as an elementary school teacher and a counselor at a psychotherapy clinic.

"I try to surround myself with people who are positive and upbeat," said Seaman. In return he tries to deal positively and hopefully with the people around him. "It's a comfortable philosophy," he told Bruce Brothers. "But that doesn't mean there are any guarantees. The cancer could come back. If it does, it does. My educational mentor, Alfred Adler, said it's not the cards we're dealt but how we play 'em."

GREAT REFERENCES

Just as every run is the product of every one you've ever taken, each book an author writes is the result of every one he has ever read. Writers were my mentors. Their advice and inspiration began long before my writing did, and continues today. This began with the first book I ever ordered from the only reliable source of running books at the time. *Track & Field News* put me in touch with my first mentor, Arthur Newton. Ten years later his photo opened my first book in recognition of his influence on it. Many more authors have contributed.

Here are my top 25 books, listed in the order read (and by original publisher and release date). Note that the youngest is a teenager now. This doesn't mean that good reading stopped in 1982, but only that the circle of mentors has become very tough to crack.

1. *Commonsense Athletics*, by Arthur Newton (Berridge, 1947). The true father of LSD.

2. *How They Train*, by Fred Wilt (Tafnews, 1959). What dozens of runners really did in training.

3. *The Four-Minute Mile*, by Roger Bannister (Dodd Mead, 1955). An autobiography bordering on poetry.

4. *How to Become a Champion*, by Percy Cerutty (Stanley Paul, 1960). An eccentric whose ideas weren't as wild as they first sounded.

5. *The Golden Mile*, by Herb Elliott (Cassell, 1961). What it took to never be beaten at this distance.

6. *Run to the Top*, by Arthur Lydiard (Jenkins, 1962). The single book that changed training the most.

7. *Loneliness of the Long Distance Runner*, by Alan Sillitoe (Allen, 1959). The classic by which all other running fiction is measured.

8. *Zatopek, the Marathon Victor*, by Frantisek Kozik (Collet's, 1955). Reveals the man behind the four gold medals.

9. *The Unforgiving Minute*, by Ron Clarke (Pelham, 1966). How he dealt with the races against time that everyone runs.

10. *Conditioning of Distance Runners*, by Tom Osler (Long

Distance Log, 1966). More good advice per page—only 32 pages here—than any other book.

11. *Jogging*, by Bill Bowerman and Waldo Harris (Grosset & Dunlap, 1967). A first attempt to apply athletic principles to fitness running.

12. *Aerobics*, by Kenneth Cooper (Evans, 1968). The launcher of the fitness revolution.

13. *My Run Across the United States*, by Don Shepherd (Tafnews, 1969). Running it with only the pack on his back to sustain him.

14. *On the Run from Dogs and People*, by Hal Higdon (Chicago Review, 1970). Humor for a sport that's often sadly lacking in it.

15. *The Zen of Running*, by Fred Rohe (Bookworks, 1974). Not as New Age mumbo-jumboish as the title suggests.

16. *Dr. Sheehan on Running*, by George Sheehan (World, 1975). His first book-length look at the question, "Why run?"

17. *The Van Aaken Method*, by Ernst Van Aaken (World, 1976). Promoted LSD with a German accent.

18. *Women's Running*, by Joan Ullyot (World, 1976). First and still the finest book on this subject.

19. *The Self-Made Olympian*, by Ron Daws (World, 1977). How smarts can sometimes win out over speed.

20. *Serious Runner's Handbook*, by Tom Osler (World, 1978). He again packed in the most advice per page.

21. *Once a Runner*, by John Parker (Cedarwinds, 1978). The truest fictional treatment of serious running.

22. *The Long Hard Road*, by Ron Hill (two volumes from Hill Sports, 1981). More detailed than any other life story.

23. *Best Efforts*, by Kenny Moore (Doubleday, 1982). The best from the sport's best writer.

24. *Galloway's Book of Running*, by Jeff Galloway (Shelter, 1982). An Olympian who speaks the common folks' language.

25. *Jackpot*, by Jim Fixx (Random House, 1982). The story behind running publishing's greatest success.

STORY OF MY LIFE

Dave Hamilton was closing in on 25 years of running without missing a day. "I'm interested in hearing about all types of streaks," he said when we met in his hometown of Portland, Oregon. "Do you have any?" Not as a runner. I once ran about five years without missing a day, but gave up that form of streaking because it undermined my running. The distances had declined, and the pains never had more than a day to go away.

Writing is a low-impact activity. I've never suffered a writing injury, so I don't need any breaks from this hobby. Long before writing became my business, I made a habit of writing a diary page each day. This is how I still start each morning, before going out to run, and then sitting down to work.

The diary streak started on April 4, 1971, after the sudden death of my father had shocked me wordless for more than a week. That day I spilled out some of the bottled-up emotion by filling five pages. This entry began with advice from my dad: "You have to do what you think is right, no matter what other people might think of you or say about you." Some would say that keeping a diary wastes writing time and energy that would be better spent on work someone would pay to read. Some would think me compulsive, but I prefer to think of it as doing what feels right.

I never dedicated the writing to my dad, an old journalist himself. I never promised myself when he died that I'd write every day from the early 1970s to the late 1990s. One day just tagged along after another, until now the days total almost 10,000 and the words several million.

What do they all mean? Very little professionally. Only a tiny percentage of this material ever passes into print. The diary isn't so much secret as it is too rough to let anyone read in this form. It isn't even training for published writing, because the two styles—public and private—differ so much. Published writing is planned, edited, polished, censored. Diary writing is unrehearsed and ad-libbed.

Edward Robb Ellis, a world-champion diarist, figures he has written 20 million words over 70 years. He says, "Writing a diary is like having a daily confrontation with the unconscious." The diary is my daily talk with myself. I sit down at dawn with no notes and little idea of what to write, and find over the next half-hour what's on my mind. I can pour it all out here without embarrassing, offending, or boring anyone.

The diary is a constant. This writing has stayed the same while the normal changes of life have swirled around me. I've passed through my high 20s to mid-50s . . . through countless up-and-down cycles in my running . . . through the sport's entire boom phase . . . through three big job changes and relocations . . . through a marriage, a divorce, and into another marriage . . . through the birth and growth of three children . . . through two minor surgeries of my own, and major ones for both wives and a daughter . . . through dozens of travels to most of the states and outside the country . . . through hundreds of magazine and newsletter columns, and many books. Through all this the diary has truly brought me back home every morning since April 1971 to continue the truest story of my life.

22

Touring the Finest Places

Each of us has favorite places to run. Places we return
to again and again. Places where running is all that it
should be. Places we wish we could be when the
setting isn't this good.

PLACES I REMEMBER

A couple of dice rolls from Reno's casinos flows the Truckee River. Alongside it lies a paved path that joined my roster of favorite places to run, along with another recent arrival. This was the seawall in Vancouver's Stanley Park, one of the most delightful meetings of land and water that you'll find in any city.

The two main raw materials of running are time and place. Together they let us put in the distance that makes us runners. We talk a lot about time—as in having enough of it (or making it), scheduling it, and running against it. But we don't talk much about place—except the mileage needed to cross it or the obstacles such as hills and traffic that it presents. Yet each of us has favorite places to run. Places we return to again and again. Places where running is all that it should be. Places we wish we could be when the setting isn't this good.

There's one preferred course in everyone's hometown. Mine is Pre's Trail in Eugene. The woodchip trail itself, named for Steve Prefontaine, runs about five miles. Mingling with the trail in this riverfront park are paved bike paths and abandoned roadways that triple the available distance. I can run here with my dog Mingo. He rarely needs to wear a leash, and we hardly ever need to run exactly the same route twice. Pre and its surroundings meet all of my requirements for a favored place to run:

- Little or no auto traffic, or noise from same as it rumbles nearby. Nothing to distract or endanger you (or your dog).

- Available for use any time, not just open on racedays or on weekends or in certain daylight hours.

- Runnable in any weather. No chance that you'll be rained or snowed out.

- Allows for at least a half-hour of running without repeats. No short laps to do.

- Requires only a few minutes' drive, if any, to reach the starting point. No sense riding for longer than you'd run.

Your town isn't likely to have a path dedicated to runners. Few do. But it probably has places that qualify as favorites based on the standards above. At least I had one in every city where I've lived.

Des Moines had Waterworks Park, into which fit most of the training miles for my first marathon. Los Altos-Mountain View had Rancho San Antonio climbing into the hills, and the Baylands levees poking into the water. The Monterey Peninsula had fire trails snaking through the 17-Mile Drive area.

I also find a special course in most of my travels. Sometimes a local host tips me off, but often I just stumble onto it. (Tip for travelers: Don't expect much help from hotel personnel. Their idea of a long run is to the next block and back. Ask another runner.) My all-time list of favorites ranges from the boardwalk in Ocean Grove, New Jersey, where George Sheehan did much of his running . . . to the river valley paths in Edmonton, Alberta, a forested gorge cutting through the heart of the city . . . to the paved beach paths extending for miles north and south of Los Angeles . . . to the Cedar Valley Trail, a converted rail line between Cedar Rapids and Waterloo, Iowa.

This list of favorites is never final. Like all runners, I'm always looking for new and better places to fill the running time.

Norm Frank

If you want to know the best places to run marathons, ask Norm Frank. He has seen most of them, as this June 1994 *Running Commentary* piece illustrates.

Norm Frank, at age 61, runs marathons almost as often as some of us train hard. He zeroed in this spring on a seemingly unbreakable record, the late Sy Mah's lifetime total of 524. To appreciate that count, think of the time and frequency needed to reach it: a marathon every week for 10 years, or one a month for 43 years, or one a year for . . . well, you get the idea.

The record now belongs to Frank, and writers David Blaikie and Jim Memmott have assured me that Frank is Sy Mah's best possible successor. Sy himself would have nominated him.

Blaikie writes in *Ultramarathon Canada* that Frank and Mah were partners in this enterprise. They ran 200 of their marathons together. Frank made a point of tying the record—but not breaking it—in Mah's old hometown of Toledo, Ohio. "I'm sure Sy would have been happy," he said. Frank waited until the next week at Buffalo to make the mark his own. This was the nearest marathon on that weekend to his hometown of Rochester.

Following the lead of his pal Mah, Frank doesn't train much between marathons or aim high in them. "I see people burn out because they train hard and set their goals too high," he tells Rochester newspaper columnist Memmott. "That never happened to me."

Frank has run more different marathons than anyone in the world. But when asked his favorite, he names "all of them." He admits to Blaikie a preference for smaller races. "I feel better about them," he says. "The people in small races do it for ordinary reasons. The atmosphere is closer to the people somehow."

Frank thinks of himself as just another runner out there entering any race he can find. "Sy and I didn't feel we were doing anything out of the ordinary," he tells Jim Memmott. "It's hard to believe that I'll be a world-record holder for something I enjoy so much."

He hasn't stopped counting at 525. He has no idea where the record might stop. "I don't have a total number I would like to run," Norm Frank says. "I never have a number. My goal is to keep doing it."

ROAD-APPLE RUN

When Anne Gault first called me about visiting this race, she described it as "a homey little event." This was by way of comparison with the Crim Races, for which she directs a cast of 15,000. Two weeks later and 200 miles to the north she assists her husband John Gault with a race on Mackinac Island. By "homey" I thought she meant it would attract a few hundred runners.

The first fact you need to know about Mackinac is how to pronounce it. The last syllable doesn't rhyme with the first. It's "Mac-in-awe." The second fact to know about this island is that it's a long way from anywhere. It's a four- or five-hour drive from the nearest metropolis, just below Michigan's Upper Peninsula where Lakes Huron and Michigan meet. The third and most critical fact to realize about Mackinac is that it's accessible only by ferryboat. On the island, travel is only by horse-drawn taxi, bike, or foot.

There's irony here: The state best known for making cars has as one of its leading tourist spots an island that bars cars. Tourists drive long distances to get here, then leave their cars behind in the jammed lots on the mainland. A motorless vacation appeals especially to runners.

As we drove toward Mackinac, I asked race announcer Scott Hubbard, "How many people does this race draw, 200 or so?" Scott said, "Try 10 times that many. The field has topped 2000 the past two years, and we're expecting at least as many this time." I could think of no place else where so many runners travel so far to reach a race. Possibly the St. George Marathon in remote southern Utah, but it's not a carless island.

The first adjustment to make when stepping onto the island is realizing that the streets and roads are yours to share only with horses, hikers, and bikers. With the usual threat banished, you don't have to hug the sidewalks and shoulders. The loudest sound here is the clomp-clomp of horses, and they travel at a pace that gently warns you to make way. The second adjustment to make here is to watch your step for a related reason. The Mackinac Island Eight-Mile could be renamed the "Road-Apple Run," so plentiful is the evidence that horses have passed this way before. A faint but not unpleasant aroma of horse wafts across the island.

I asked Scott Hubbard where we would run on Mackinac. Without cars, would there be enough miles of roads as we know them? Would we follow horse and bike trails? Scott described the back-island roads, paved but narrower than normal—only about one lane wide. This requires starting the race in four waves, two minutes apart, to ease congestion.

"The course isn't hard to follow," Scott added. "It circles the island once, for eight miles, and you don't need a map. Just keep the lake on your left." This course was one of the best I've run. It's worth a trip from anywhere.

LITTLE GIANTS

Twice in two weeks the same question brought the same answer. "I want to run a spring marathon on the West Coast," both runners said. "Which do you recommend?" Both times I named the Avenue of the Giants in northern California. It's both less and more than we've come to expect from modern marathons.

The Avenue's entrants number in the hundreds, not the thousands. The race offers no brass bands, no crowds lining the course. But it does offer more to look at than almost any other marathon.

Runners who claim that scenery doesn't matter, or they're too busy to notice, haven't seen The Avenue (or the Humboldt Redwoods Marathon, run on the same road later each year).

This is the finest marathon course I've ever run. A freeway bypassed this narrow road, leaving the original to slow-moving vehicles and slower-moving pedestrians. The whole course passes under trees hundreds of years old and hundreds of feet tall. They shade the road into semidarkness.

The redwoods also distort the senses. So quiet is the forest that while running there I could hear conversations of other runners a quarter-mile away. So massive are the trees that I seemed to pass them in slow motion. I don't freely toss out the word "spiritual." But this might be the most spiritual place I've ever visited. You can't come here without feeling moved by living beings so old and so large. Dozens of generations of humans have hurried past while these trees looked on.

© Ken Lee

When the Avenue of the Giants Marathon turned 25, I pulled out my story written after race number one. That piece held up to the years better than most do. It praised The Avenue much the same way I do now. It began, "Runners continually talk of The Perfect Marathon, hinting that like perfect love or perfect happiness it is something they can't quite find. Maybe it's this search for elusive perfection that drives them on. Well, I just ran The Perfect Marathon and have mixed feelings about it. I'm glad I did it, but I'm wondering too what's left now." Certainly no more sub-three-hour marathons. I'd hit that target in about half of my previous marathons, but never would again.

The 1972 story was titled "Three Hours in Paradise." It ended with some off-base prophecy: "If you're thinking of running here next year, don't count on it. The California Parks Department extracted a large sum from the race promoters for a $100,000 insurance policy. Entry fees didn't begin to pay for it, so this may have been the first and last Avenue of the Giants Marathon. Paradise lost. It was nice while it lasted."

It has lasted another 25-plus years. Think about running here sometime to feel humbled in age and size among the ancient giants, and honored to move through one of nature's finest cathedrals.

TRAIL OF DREAMS

My running started here, in an Iowa town that is but a pinprick on the state map. I came back one summer for a high school reunion. The group was small enough, just 10 of us, that each could speak for several minutes on where life had taken him or her since we last met. I said, "I've never grown up. I'm still doing what I did 35 years ago." Others played sports in high school, then set them aside. They moved on to farming, building, trucking, teaching, and preaching.

I ran then and run now. But I feel oddly self-conscious doing it where it all began. It's as if the people who knew me first and best are staring and asking, "Why's an old guy like you still doing this?" It's as if I'd never gotten over playing hide-and-seek, or its local variation that we called "chalk the corner."

So when I go back to Coin, Iowa, I do what I'd never think of doing at my current home or in any other travels. I hide. I drive to the countryside—a very short distance in Coin—to run almost unseen on the farm roads. The sight of another runner here would surprise me, too.

At the school reunion I talked with the event's organizer, a woman named Connie who once lived across the street from us. She'd stayed in town as a teacher. "Did you run today?" asked Connie. That's a better question than, Do you still run? "Oh sure," I told her. "But I didn't see anyone else out there."

She said I didn't go out at the right time or look hard enough. "I've run for the past 10 years, and I'm not the only one who does it." She named several other adults, along with the best of the young runners. This girl Sarah, who grew up on a nearby farm, had won a college scholarship in track.

I saw Sarah's dad, Phil, at the reunion. He said, "She's working this summer on the Wabash Trace." My heart leaped. For years I'd heard that the long-abandoned Wabash railroad bed would become a hiking-biking trail—available, of course, for running if anyone cared to use it that way. It was meant to pass between Omaha and Kansas City, with Coin at about its midpoint. I thought the project had died from lack of funding or interest, but Phil now said otherwise. "It's already finished from just north of town all the way to Omaha. They're extending it south this summer to the Missouri line."

Our reunion ran late into the night, but I still ran early the next morning. Couldn't wait to test the Trace. No other runners appeared during my time on this trail—not even any hikers or bikers. But that doesn't mean they don't or won't appear here.

"Build it," said the Iowa-filmed movie *Field of Dreams,* "and they will come." Offer runners the trail of our dreams, and we will find it.

23

Connecting With Other Runners

You can't get a real feel for a race from TV coverage,

or from reading newspapers and magazines (and now

the Internet), or even from standing along the course

watching. To know it you must do it. The race is the

best place to stay in touch with the most people.

CAMP FOLLOWER

Say "running camp" to someone who has never attended one, and the first image that jumps to mind is "boot camp." Reveille at dawn, day-long workouts, meals in a mess hall, nights in a barracks, mandatory attendance at all scheduled activities, roll calls, drill instructors, and discipline. Only a seriously crazed runner would pay to be treated like this.

I'm a committed camp follower. I can assure you that none of the running camps I've attended is anything like boot camp. I've been with Jeff Galloway at one of his camps every summer since 1980, most of them at Lake Tahoe. He prefers the term *fitness vacation* to free it of the military imagery, but it remains "running camp" to the campers. And so the confusion remains over what they do here.

Jeff conducts several camps, in the United States and abroad. This one comes to Squaw Valley, California, for a week each summer. Campers are lodged in condos designed to satisfy well-off skiers during their season. Meals are served in a nearby restaurant, where the usual clientele is equally demanding.

The running possibilities at Squaw Valley, home of the 1960 Winter Olympics and starting line for the Western States 100, as well as at the nearby lakeshore, are varied and attractive. But Jeff schedules only one group run most days, plus an afternoon hike, and these aren't required of anyone. The guest speakers are plentiful, and they fill two to three hours each day. But no one checks on who does or doesn't show up here, or who stays awake during the talks.

The vital center of this camp isn't the running/hiking routes or the lecture rooms. It's Le Chamois restaurant. My favorite part of this annual stay is the meals, and not for the food (which is generous and tasty) but for the talk. We runners don't usually talk enough with each other. Races turn us inside ourselves, and training runs are more often private than social. We talk best while sitting still, which we rarely take time to do together at home. A camp like this brings us together to sit and eat—and mealtime is the one activity here with perfect attendance.

The campers linger over their meals for an hour or two. I make a point of sitting with different tablemates at each meal, trying to talk with all 40 in the group at some time during the stay. At mealtime I catch up on the news of the old-timers. Joe from

Tennessee and Dexter from Georgia tell of becoming grandfathers since our visit here last year; two of the new parents had come to this camp as kids. Judi and John from the Bay Area report on their recent wedding day, when they ran Bay to Breakers with John in a wedding gown and Judi a tux.

I get to know the newcomers. Dr. Elmo, a veterinarian in San Francisco, tells of moonlighting as a musician (and, by request, later performs his comedy hit, "Grandma Got Run Over by a Reindeer"). I ask Ginny from Florida when she began running, and she says, "When I got here." This was Ginny's version of boot camp. It was far from a Camp Pendleton and close to a Club Med.

PROS AT WORK

This was a business trip for the visiting professionals. They were beginning the last and hardest lap of their weekend. Local runners who made up nearly all of the race field the day before were home asleep in their own beds. The pros were up early to head toward faraway homes. This was the morning after the race, when the pros hit emotional and physical lows to balance off the highs of the day before. These runners were leaving town before the sun came up, and they'd had no time for an eye-opening run.

In this case, the town was Flint, Michigan, where they raced the Crim 10-mile. In a week or two they would join the nomadic pro running circuit someplace else. None of the passengers in the back seat was speaking now. They wished the driver and his front-seat passengers, a TV producer and a writer, would stop yakking and let them doze. One of the pros tried not to become ill. All of them tried not to think about the violent thunderstorm they would soon fly through.

Two men in the back seat were past winners here, with four titles between them. One finished out of the money this time, and the other didn't finish at all. Brian Sheriff is a citizen of the world— son of a Zimbabwean mother and Irish-American father, college educated in the United States and working in Japan for Mazda. Sheriff flew halfway around the world, only to eat something at his prerace meal that made him ill. He finished a distressed 18th. Getting into the car the next morning to start his trip back to Osaka, he said, "Give me a window seat. I feel even worse today and might need to make a quick stop."

Ken Martin was newly remarried and resettled in Colorado. He'd come to Flint looking for the form that had won this race for him twice before. Martin dropped out and wound up in the medical tent. "There's nothing really wrong with me," he said later. "I'm just having trouble racing for some reason."

Both Sheriff and Martin lost the gamble that goes with being a running pro. They missed out on the cash. There are no guaranteed paydays in prize-money races. The bigger the purse, the more competitive the races become and the greater the odds of being shut out.

Running for a living isn't as lucrative or as glamorous as it appears when we catch glimpses of the pros at the starting line, on the awards stand, and in news coverage. I sometimes get more revealing looks. I wandered uninvited into a heated discussion at Flint between race officials and a woman from a country, Serbia,

© Photo Run/Victah Sailer

Anne-Marie Lauck.

where seventh-place money goes a long way. She was about to lose it all for cutting corners.

Even winners don't get away easily. I stood in the long line of reporters wanting to interview Anne Marie Lauck. She looked more relieved by than elated with her victory. She'd moved to Atlanta that summer to adapt to heat, yet had required medical treatment after becoming overheated in the Falmouth race. Lauck won Crim six days later, then hobbled into the interview area with blood seeping from her shoes. She said, "I might be overtraining for the New York City Marathon. I ran a slower time today than my 10-mile split will need to be at New York." She would have preferred to get out of the sun and off her feet, to shower and eat as other runners do. But Lauck carried through with the postrace obligations of being a winner. These take longer than the race, and this is when a pro earns her money.

STAYING IN TOUCH

If you like your running commentary hot, try the newsletter *Running, Ranting, and Racing*. It's as spicy as mine is mild. *RRR* names names in its critical comment. For instance, one issue pointed out Amby Burfoot's and Jeff Galloway's slow running at the Boston Marathon.

I won't try to reproduce the tone of that item. The gist of it: Why would these well-known runners-turned-writers settle for being so . . .well, average in a setting as public as Boston's 100th running? Why would Burfoot, who had once won Boston and come within a second of the American marathon record, take almost twice as long to finish this year? Or why would Galloway, who'd once run 2:15 and competed in the Olympics, take more than five hours at Boston?

I know both men and what their answers would be. They had better things to do that day than to run fast. Amby chose to run with his wife, Cristina Negron. It was their first Boston as a married couple, and they wanted to spend it together. This was Jeff's 100th marathon, and he chose to run it with his 75-year-old father, Elliott Galloway. Jeff called it "one of the two or three greatest moments in my career."

I also offer a more general answer as to why anyone with nothing left to prove would race so much more slowly than he once did. I'm one of those people. My racing is now so average that it's almost invisible. "Do you still run races?" I am asked by people who never see me hidden in these crowds.

One answer is, "I have to run races. My writing life depends on it." You can't write books and articles for participants without participating. You can't tell what it's like inside the sport without being an insider. You can't get a real feel for a race from TV coverage, or from reading newspapers and magazines (and now the Internet), or even from standing along the course watching. To know it you must do it.

During a spell of shaky health I passed through one of my longest droughts, going six months without running a race. I felt badly disconnected—from the sport, yes, but more from my racing friends. I need to join them. Not as a writer or a speaker or a commentator, but as someone whose job doesn't mean a thing on this day. I don't just have to be here but want to be, no matter how long the running takes.

The race is the best place to stay in touch with the most people. Or, as Amby Burfoot and Jeff Galloway did at Boston, to share something this big with one partner.

Kim Jones

Jones, a professional runner, has kept a sense of balance in her life. I profiled her in the October 1996 *Running Commentary*.

Kim Jones is 38 years old and the mother of two. Both daughters were born before she won her first national marathon title, in 1986. As we rode together to the Detroit airport, she wanted to talk as much about her younger daughter as about her own running.

"Jamie ran track as a freshman this year," said Kim. "She ran the 800 in 2:17 and made the final at the state meet. Then she got to go with me to the Track Trials in Atlanta."

"Yes, I saw you run there," I told her. "What inspired that?" She was typecast as a marathoner, having run in three World Championships as well as placing second at New York City twice and Boston once. But she'd also dropped out of the last two Olympic Marathon Trials with injury and illness. Her asthma, which attacks unpredictably in long races, has become increasingly worrisome.

"After my disappointment in Columbia," said Kim of the 1996 Marathon Trial, "I wanted to try something entirely different." She dropped from the marathon on the roads in February to 5000 meters on the track in June.

"I chose this race instead of the 10,000 because I was afraid that my asthma would kick in during the 10," she said. "The breathing problems don't usually start for 15 minutes or so, and I could get through the 5000 in that time." Kim wasn't a speedless roadie. She had been nationally ranked in the 800 in high school, but the track 5000 was a new distance to her this spring.

"I was partly doing this for the road runners," she told me. This was her answer to

© Ken Lee

track people who think that marathoners never had any turnover or had it pounded out of them by the roads. Her daughter Jamie's new career on the track influenced Kim's return as well. This was a sport they could still share. "She came within one second of what I ran in the 800 at the same age," said the proud mom.

The daughter felt great pride this summer, too, as she watched Kim place seventh in the Trials 5000. Few other high school athletes have ever seen a parent come this close to making an Olympic team.

GIVING THANKS

George Sheehan wrote so well that even his rejects sang. *Runner's World* turned down an essay of his, not because the writing was flawed but only because he said so little about running. George wrote there about the fine, often lost art of saying thank you. "We runners are a self-centered lot," he began. "In our preoccupation with performance at races, we don't often pause to think about who made the racing possible or take time to thank all concerned."

He pointed an accusing finger at himself in this setting. "I'm no better than anyone else. I should say thanks at every water station, to every traffic guard, to the people at the chute, and end by thanking the race director, yet I rarely do." George handed out thank-yous more freely while going about his everyday business. "Why thank people who have just done their job?" he wrote. "The answer, it seems to me, is that the thank-you completes the action of being served. Giving thanks is the role of the recipient. When the donor is not thanked, when good wishes and good words don't go from heart to heart, a chain in human interaction is broken."

George wrote this essay for Thanksgiving, "a day on which we thank the Lord for His blessings. It should also be a day when we stop, then think, then thank our fellow human beings." We don't need to wait for one special day to say our thank-yous. Recognizing they're never, never out of season, I thank:

- George Sheehan, who is my most constant friend and teacher.

- Writers like George whose words I quote (with credit) when they say things better than I can.

- Other friends who forgive me for avoiding them when I run and write.

- Wife and children who never ask, "Why don't you go to an office during the week and stay home on weekends like other dads?"

- Parents and siblings who never pushed me into what I do now, but have always supported these odd habits.

- The people at *Runner's World* who continue to support me while hardly ever seeing me at work.

- Book buyers who pay the ultimate compliment of paying to read these pages.

- Readers who generally don't exaggerate either their praise or criticism of the writing.

- Letter writers who get slow or no replies, even though I do read every letter when it arrives and intend to answer it someday.

- Hosts who make me feel at home when I'm away from home twice each month.

- Anonymous volunteers and spectators who make the roads smoother at races.

- Experts who keep coming up with new advice to write about and to try.

- "Name" runners who still have the power to excite me with their speed, long after mine has vanished.

Finally I give thanks that running remains as enjoyable in the 40th year as it was in the first.

24

Voicing a Few Complaints

Imagine if you were running an out-and-back
course—at night—with no other runners and
no spectators in sight. Would you turn back
anywhere from a block to a mile early? No one
else would know, but your knowing would be
punishment enough.

LITTLE IRRITANTS

I had to laugh that the *Los Angeles Times* asked me, of all people, to critique the movie *Prefontaine*. I'm no critic. I prefer to look for the good instead of reporting the bad. But I took on the *Times* assignment and had the article bounced back to me twice for rewrites because it wasn't tough enough. Then a few runner-readers criticized me for being too tough on the movie. One reader said, "This isn't like you."

No, it's not. I don't go out of my way to run down the sport and its practitioners, and more often err in the opposite direction by singing their praises too loudly. This might leave you thinking that I must like everyone who runs and everything about running. Not quite. In the interests of realism and balance, I give you the following list of little irritants in the life of this runner. But the Pollyanna in me can't help adding that enduring these few negatives add to the appreciation of the many positives. What I don't like about running:

The first mile of most runs, before you find a rhythm . . . Running in darkness when each foot plant is an act of faith . . . Times unreadable in the dark without holding the watch six inches from your face . . . Looking down in midrun and seeing the watch still reading "0:00" . . . Looking down after a time trial to find the watch still running . . . People who ask for the time of day when you're in stopwatch mode . . . Ending a run early and walking back to the start, even when injury control demands it . . . Courses that start downhill and beat up a cold body . . . Courses that finish uphill and beat down an already tired body . . . Courses that pass the eventual finish line before you're finished.

Waiting for stoplights to change . . . Waiting for traffic to pass before you cross a street . . . Jumping on and off curbs . . . Oncoming drivers who won't dim their lights for a mere pedestrian . . . Drivers who don't signal their turns for you, coast through stop signs, won't yield an inch of their lane on an otherwise empty road, or drive in the bike lane . . . Bikers startling you as they silently pass from behind . . . Unseen dogs that first bark when you're three feet away . . . A pebble inside the shoe that feels like a boulder . . . A rock stuck in the shoe tread and scraping along the road . . . Stepping on gum or dog poop on the sidewalk . . . Stinky shoes from running without socks . . . Slipping into clammy shoes that haven't dried out from the last run or the last wash . . . Shoes that disappear from the market as soon as they become favorites.

Running in long pants that seem to restrict leg motion even if they don't . . . Cold hands and ears that make you feel cold all over . . . Finishing into a headwind . . . Sudden rain showers that catch you underdressed . . . Invisible patches of ice on the streets that lurk to tackle you . . . Being seen walking, even if you believe in the value of walking breaks . . . Getting caught making a pit stop, even when you tried to be discreet . . . Spit and snot that end up on your chin, cheek or chest . . . Sloshing of food or water in the belly . . . Swallowing a bug or catching one in the eye.

Walkers who hog the inside lane of the track while you're running there for time . . . The looks of business-suited travelers when you walk into a hotel elevator in few clothes and a full sweat . . . Greeting another runner and not getting so much as eye contact in return . . . Tailgating runners who attach themselves to your pace when you want to run alone . . . Watching healthy runners race when you're unwell and can't run.

WHO'S CHEATING WHOM?

When I hear of runners cheating in a race, pretending to do what they didn't, stealing an honor that wasn't theirs, I'm as amazed as I am appalled. This crime is foreign to everything most runners believe. If we run mostly to improve and impress ourselves, then the person most cheated is the cheater. Thousands of runners honored the pledge to themselves to run an honest race one spring at the Boston and Pittsburgh marathons. A few deviants couldn't accept the elemental honesty of a certain time over a specific distance.

A husband-wife couple "won" their age groups at Boston, and a man snuck into seventh place in Pittsburgh's national-championship division. John Murphy, 64, and Suzanne Murphy, 59, from California, claimed to have run 2:43 and 3:12 at Boston. Scott Stakich, a 23-year-old from Pennsylvania, briefly got away with breaking 2:20 at Pittsburgh. I could have refused to type their names, treating them as the nonfinishers they were and antirunners they are. But greater good may be done by naming them. This might shame them permanently from the sport and deter others tempted to try the same dirty deeds.

If the Murphys and Stakich really believe what they did, they have simple recourse. They can clear their names without going to court but by running another carefully monitored race and coming anywhere near their claimed time. History says they won't. Others caught cheating in some of America's biggest races—Rosie Ruiz, Candy Dodge, Frank Grey, John Bell, Oscar Miranda, and their ilk—all protested their innocence. But all failed to make amends in the one way that any runner would accept.

I won't overstate the problem. Cheaters are as rare in this sport as sub-2:20 American marathoners. But one scofflaw per thousand honorable runners is too many, and surveillance must be vigorous and punishment harsh to root out that one. When the Murphys and Stakich were nabbed, they raised further suspicions: How often had they gotten away with this before? And how many others do the same and avoid detection?

If secret on-course videotaping or computer-chip technology catch cheaters, what is fitting punishment? A lifetime ban from racing, certainly (though this is usually voluntary, since the exposed seldom show their faces at races again). Banishment isn't enough. My friend Geoff Pietsch, once the victim of a cheater at the New York City Marathon, says, "I'd personally favor drawing and quartering, but would settle for jail time. Why shouldn't someone who steals another's achievements—honors which matter far more than worldly goods—go to jail?"

Maybe the real age-group winners at Boston, Anthony Cerminaro and Susan Gustafson, should have sued the Murphys. Or maybe officials in Pittsburgh should have charged Stakich with trying to make off with $2500 that wasn't his (including temporarily picking $500 from the pocket of the real seventh-placer, Michael Dudley).

I'd settle for the cheaters sitting down with a tough interviewer who asks how they would explain themselves to the runners they defrauded, or to their families, or to themselves. They'd have excuses, of course, that let them live with their lies. A shriveled conscience separates the shortcutters from you and me.

Imagine if you were running an out-and-back course . . . at night . . . with no other runners and no spectators in sight . . . no official or video camera at the turnaround . . . no computer chip in your shoelace. Would you turn back anywhere from a block to a mile early? No one else would know, but your knowing would be punishment enough.

Jacqueline Gareau

© Photo Run/Victah Sailer

She was once the victim of the sport's most notorious cheater, but rose far above Rosie. I wrote about Gareau in the November 1996 *Running Commentary*.

You might think that with all my travels through the sport for all these years, I would have bumped into most of running's big names. Not so. I've missed more of these athletes than I have met. One who got away until this fall was Jacqueline Gareau. We finally talked at the Royal Victoria Marathon, where she was a featured speaker and the honored guest at the prerace dinner.

It was Jacqueline who crossed the Boston Marathon finish line in 1980 behind the woman whose name we still can't utter without gagging. Jacqueline was belatedly honored as the first, and still only, Canadian woman to win at Boston. She comes from Quebec, taught herself English as an adult, and now speaks the second language fluently but still is shy about going public in it. She came to her Victoria talk armed with a thick stack of index cards, carefully printed and color coded so the words would come out right. She then talked easily about her running life, seldom glancing at the cue cards.

She told of starting to run for exercise (at age 24) and making a marathon her first race (finishing in about 3:40). She would improve by more than an hour. Jacqueline ran in the first World Championships Marathon for women, placing fifth. But her three Olympic attempts brought frustration and then joy. She dropped out with an injury at the Los Angeles Games. Three Canadian women ran faster

219

in 1988 and bumped her off the Seoul team. She was training for a final Olympic attempt in 1992 when she learned she was pregnant for the first time at age 39. She says of her now four-year-old son, "He is my gold medal."

Jacqueline Gareau is the Joan Benoit Samuelson of Canada. The country's most successful woman marathoner, yes, but also a ground breaker. Today's U.S. women marathoners honor Samuelson for making this road easier for them to take. At the Victoria dinner honoring Gareau, a speaker asked, "All you Canadian women who are running the marathon tomorrow, please stand and applaud this woman who made it easier for you to be here." About 100 of them stood and cheered, and Jacqueline responded, "My heart fills with love for you all."

GARBAGE MILES

A few runners lead, and the rest of us follow them. For a short while early in my running life, I was a leader in some small-time races. Now I'm a follower, from ever-wider distances as age moves me back through the pack. Slowing has its advantages. It put me with a bigger and more varied group of runners than I once saw while trying to distance myself from all followers.

But following more and more people also has its downside. It shows me what everyone ahead left behind while passing this way earlier. The leaders never see the gloves and garbage bags that overdressed runners discard in the early miles, never wade through the drifts of paper cups at aid stations, never—and here's our latest environmental insult—find an energy-food wrapper glued to their shoes. Runners like to think of ourselves as environmentalists. We want our air untainted and our ground uncluttered. The casual messing up of our surroundings disgusts us. We get worked up over the bad breath of traffic and the smokers who toss aside their smoldering butts.

Environmental activists grow like weeds in the area where I now live, the Pacific Northwest. I don't normally join their chorus, but seeing evidence of the slob problem on my running routes does make me see red. Once I found a discarded plastic bag along a forest path. Inside were the culprit's name and address. I stuffed some of the garbage inside one of his own envelopes and mailed it to him with a note: "Don't trash our trail!"

Oddly, these sensitivities too often shut down when runners line up for races. Suddenly we seem to expect mom or someone to clean up after us. Runners who would glare or shout at drinkers who litter the roadsides with beer cans or burger boxes become litterers themselves at races. The latest and most insidious culprit among the marathoners that I follow is PowerBar and PowerGel packaging.

Please don't think I'm picking on the products themselves. I mention these two by name because they are the leaders in their class of energy boosters. I applaud Brian Maxwell for all he has done at PowerFood Inc. He's one of us, a former marathoner and a good one, who has built a healthy business around the leathery bars and gooey gels.

I'm a latecomer to using them after spending too many years running hungry. The bars, which I adopted for races and long runs in 1994, work well to reduce late-miles energy crises. The gels, which I started using only last year, work even better if only because they go down easier. The longer the run, the more effective these products are. Marathoners in particular swear by them—and marathon directors swear at them, because of the resulting litter.

One director pleaded with me recently, "Can you write something that makes runners aware of this growing problem?" Happy to. The problem isn't with the products, whose manufacturers have to package them in something inedible and want to see it disposed of cleanly. No, we're the problem. Runners who couldn't imagine tossing a candy wrapper out their car window think nothing of dropping gel or bar packaging along a race course.

But we drop our cups at drink stations, you might say. What's the difference? Big difference: Aid stations come at prescribed locations and are staffed with volunteers who clean up cups from the next hundred yards or so. They rake or kick the cups into a pile for quick collection.

Runners can rip into bars or squeeze down gels anywhere along the course. Then too many of us leave the wrappings behind—usually with no official workers stationed nearby. Even near drink stops, the sticky packets glue themselves to the road and defy easy pickup.

The solution couldn't be simpler. We carried these energy products this far, in a fanny pack or (in my case) a sandwich baggy. How tough is it to stuff our garbage back where it came from?

RAIN ON OUR PARADE

Here in the Pacific Northwest, where I live and run, we don't dream of a white Christmas but expect a wet one. Rain falls regularly and often heavily here from shortly after Labor Day to almost the Fourth of July. So while we know less than most of you about dressing for the cold and snow, we know what to wear—and not wear—on rainy days. If you don't run in rain here, you don't run for half the year.

At one marathon that I attended, a storm rolled through on race eve. This panicked one man, who checked out of his hotel at two o'clock in the morning and later mailed back his race number, demanding a refund because officials couldn't guarantee him a dry run. In fact, raceday was dry. But even the slight possibility of rain caused another runner to wear the high-priced rainsuit he'd

bought the day before. He soon overheated and handed the suit to a stranger beside the course—and later demanded that officials retrieve it for him.

I visited another marathon that had enjoyed a streak of dry years. Now rain was forecast, and a main topic of discussion at the Saturday expo was, "What should I wear?" The office was showered with calls asking, "Will the race be canceled if it rains?" The rain blew in overnight and stayed through marathon Sunday. It truly was a bad day—for standing and watching. Officials who honored their commitment and spectators without a good excuse to stay home looked miserable.

But it wasn't a bad day for running. Temperatures were mild, winds gentle, rains light. No one would freeze or melt. Runners who weren't at home in these conditions started the race in the garbage bags they'd worn to the start. One man wrapped his head and neck, one knee and both feet in clear plastic bags.

Many runners reacted as if they were about to sail with the fishing fleet into a typhoon. Some wore coats, pants, and gloves. They later looked like human clotheslines as they draped stripped-off items from their waists and necks, or littered the roadside with enough clothing to stock a Goodwill store. They forgot some truisms of running: If you feel comfortable while standing at the starting line, you'll soon be too warm . . . . The apparent temperature warms up by 20 degrees during a run . . . . It's better to underdress than overdress.

Before leaving our hotel for the race, I had told my wife Barbara, "This would be the day of my dreams if I were running a marathon." Most of my best road-race times have come on days like this, when nature's air-conditioning is set at ideal. This day I ran half a marathon, and at a pace that wouldn't build up much steam. Yet I wore only the usual shorts and T-shirt. The one concession to the rain was a cap to keep the drops off my glasses.

Take it from a longtime moss-backed, wet-footed runner: The widespread fear of rain is exaggerated and the contempt for it misplaced. Rain seldom spoils anything about a race except how you look in the finish-line photo.

25

Singing the Sport's Praises

We need to promote what Our Sport is instead of apologizing for what it isn't. It isn't and may never be a high-ratings media attraction, but its strength is in its numbers of participants. Our tribe keeps growing, whether the outside media choose to pay attention or not.

CHANGING OUR WORLD

Having passed through the decades of the 1950s to the 1990s as a runner, I can say that the best time to run is now. Never have there been more runners, and never has running left bigger marks on society at large.

While ambling through the park in supposedly mean inner-city Los Angeles, the thought struck me: Running has truly changed the world. Note that I didn't say saved the world. I'm not one who claims this sport can cure everything from bad breath to nuclear war. Running has made our world a little more safe and comfortable. The many runners streaming through this park deter the bad guys who might prey on anyone here alone.

Here are nine ways that running has improved our world:

1. Running reinvented the shoe. It made foot-friendly shoes fashionable. Running shoes—then aerobics, cross-training, and basketball shoes—became the casual footwear of choice, even for people who only exercise their egos.

2. Running changed the way we dress. It made "sweats" acceptable wear, not only for workouts but also for the supermarket. Our sport first adopted miracle fibers such as Lycra, polypro, and Gore-Tex, and then exported them to the population at large.

3. Running made it okay again for adults to use the streets without wheels under them. Before the running boom the only adults who ran on the streets were trying to catch buses. The only ones who walked were those who couldn't afford cars or cab fare.

4. Running made the country fitter, or at least more fitness-minded. Dr. Kenneth Cooper's aerobics program had its roots in our sport because Cooper was a longtime runner, and most of his early converts followed his example by running.

5. Running led the way for its offshoots. It opened the roads to walkers and bicyclists. It spun off the triathlon. It fueled a boom in cross-country skiing and spawned the water-training alternative.

6. Running welcomed women and the old. It was the first sport to treat them as equals with the men and the young. It's still one of the few sports in which both sexes and all ages train and compete side by side.

7. Running came up with the idea that "everyone's a winner." It invented the PR as a personal definition of winning. It pioneered the concept that participating beats watching, and that finishing with your own best effort can be just as rewarding as finishing first.

8. Running promoted preventive medicine. It showed that we could take charge of our own health—from avoiding injuries to improving diet to easing stress—instead of depending on doctors to clear away the damage of neglect.

9. Running made the world a little cleaner. Every runner saw and felt the earth up close and breathed the air unfiltered. Each one became more of an environmentalist.

LET RUNNING BE

Here's a story I wish I'd written. I don't know its writer, Bill Gray, and don't read his magazine, *Tennis.* But with a few word changes, his lines are a perfect fit with running. Hal Higdon, whose son David is a tennis player and writer, faxed me Gray's column. It began, "I don't know about you, but I'm through apologizing for Our Game because it isn't a mass-consumption sport and doesn't have a Tiger in its tank to fuel it into 21st-century mega-popularity. And I'm weary of the outside mass media crowing about Our Game's 'demise.'"

Gray then commended Nike (which happens to be a fueler of megasports) for its ad titled "Let Tennis Be Tennis." The column quoted Nike's Skip Lei: "We started looking introspectively at the game through our eyes as recreational tennis players, and decided we're no-way going to make excuses for our sport. Instead we're going to celebrate the people who play it. They're our evangelists, and it's their enthusiasm that will spark new people to come into our game."

Gray decried attempts "to make Our Game more like the other games . . . . We're not like the other games. What team-sports fans and the outside media that obsessively cover other games don't understand is our unique culture. In tennis we'd rather play Our Game than watch it lying down like the team-sports couch potatoes."

The same could be said for Our Sport, running. Nike would do well to launch a parallel advertising campaign stating boldly and at the top, "Let Running Be Running." Or maybe USATF, under the guidance of running-wise and media-savvy Craig Masback, could take up this call. Work to streamline and modernize the sport, to be sure. Grind off its rough edges accumulated in the last 30 years, certainly. But at the same time recognize all that's right about Our Sport instead of dwelling always on the few things that are wrong. Don't try to make running over in the image of the megapopular sports, because ours isn't like any of them.

Ours has less in common with ESPN SportCenter favorites football and basketball, baseball and hockey than with . . . well, tennis, since the comparison allows me to use more of Bill Gray's lines. I wish I'd said this as well, but failing that I shamelessly borrow from him: "The reason few of us tune in live to the French and Wimbledon finals [translation for runners: World Track Championships and New York City Marathon] is that most of us are on the courts [roads] on those weekend mornings—playing tennis [running] . . . . We don't really care who wins [the big events], which is impossible for team-sports fans to understand, especially those who slip into clinical depressions when their team loses the Super Bowl."

Runners aren't uninterested in what Gray called "the high priests and priestesses" of Our Sport. Yet our mental state doesn't ride with their latest results, but with our own. This is a lot healthier than worshiping the performances of strangers.

We need to promote what Our Sport is instead of apologizing for what it isn't. It isn't and may never be a high-ratings media attraction, but its strength is in its numbers of participants. Our tribe keeps growing, whether the outside media choose to pay attention or not.

SWEET NOTHINGS

Watching the mass-consumption sports—and I'm a casual follower of several—reminds me of how different they are from running. Few if any sports have less to offer than ours, and this is what I like best about it. Look at all that road racing doesn't have:

- No balls or sticks. No one hits or throws anything. Here the action centers on people, not objects.

- No time outs. Once a race starts, it doesn't stop for commercials or any other excuse.

- No overtime. A race ends at its finish line, with no one ever asked to go the extra mile to settle a score.

- No scoring. Racing results aren't figured by points but are a simple matter of time.

- No substitutions. A weary runner can't call for relief, and an eager but less talented one doesn't have to warm the bench.

- No cuts. Runners are never told to clean out their lockers and not to come back because they aren't good enough.

- No teams. There's no one to hold you back when you're running well, and no one to carry you when you're doing poorly.

- No sex separation. In football or baseball the men play and the women lead cheers. In running they all race at once.

- No referees. At least none in striped shirts who can blow a whistle during a race and assess a penalty on the spot.

- No rules. At least none more complicated than filing an entry, starting at a scheduled time and place, and staying on the course for the full distance.

- No fighting. When was the last time you saw two runners stop in midrace and settle an argument with their fists?

- No stadiums. Spectators don't sit in box seats. They stand beside the streets.

- No ticket sales. Spectators don't pay to watch the runners. Runners pay to entertain the fans.

- No crowds. Boston and New York City marathons aside, rare is the road race where the fans outnumber the runners.

- No booing. People who watch our sport from the sidelines don't act on the urge to verbally abuse a runner they don't like.

- No betting. Las Vegas publishes no "line" on our events, and no office pools ride on the results.

- No off-season. We never have to wait six months for the races to start again; there's always one next week, somewhere.

- No one winner. When winning means meeting personal standards, a race has as many potential winners as it has entrants.

- No clear losers. When losing means falling short of personal standards, the first finisher can "lose" and the last one can "win."

- No retirement. Runners never need to quit as they grow older and slower, and rarely do. They can always feel young again within a few years by graduating into a new age group.

Walt Stack

He's one of my all-time favorite characters in running. His story in the March 1995 *Running Commentary* will tell you why.

Walt Stack and San Francisco were made for each other. He might not have become a civic treasure anywhere but here, in a city that not only tolerates quirky behavior but celebrates it. Walt was a character, even by San Francisco standards. When he died at age 87, the city's two newspapers gave this avowed Communist and lifelong hard laborer a send-off befitting a statesman.

© Ken Lee

Walt's workouts were legendary, and perhaps mildly exaggerated. He was said to rise at three or four o'clock, run for two or three hours, swim a mile or two—then bike to work at a construction site. This routine began in his late 50s, and he ran dozens of marathons and ultras in the next 30 years.

I remember him less for his performances than for his personality. He was loud and profane, but had the charm to get away with it. He once said, "You can get by with saying almost anything if you say it with a smile."

Walt did lots of smiling as a runner who never took his efforts too seriously. "All this work I'm doing, it don't mean shit," he liked to say. "I'm going to croak, just like the rest of you."

When Walt founded the Dolphin-South End Runners Club, he chose a turtle as its symbol. Its motto: "Start slow and then taper off." He liked to poke fun at his own slowness. I still quote his old line about being stuck at one pace: "If they dropped me out of an airplane, I would fall at $8\frac{1}{2}$ minutes a mile." After one laborious race, he voiced a classic description of hitting the wall: "I'm going to sue the city for building the road too close to my ass."

Walt, who refused to discuss politics on the run, said, "You can be a real Bircher, I can be a Communist, and I can still love you because I figure you're a runner. You're a good Joe, and you'll feel the same way about me. You'll say, 'Geez, he's a dirty Red, but he's Walt Stack. He's a runner. He's my buddy.'" Walt was a buddy to every runner who ever met him. I'm proud to have been one among those thousands.

FORWARD THINKING

It comes with age, of course. The older we get, the greater the shift in proportions from life ahead of us to the living behind us, the more we look back and the less ahead. These days writing sometimes overflows with backward thinking . . . . No, that doesn't sound right. Make it nostalgia. You might think from reading these pieces that I'm ready to take up residence on a bar stool, and from there to bore people with how things used to be and how they've gone to hell since then. But I haven't sunk that low quite yet.

Blame some of what you see on these pages on my chosen profession. Journalists mainly write about the past. It's the nature of our work to review what already has happened rather than anticipate what's to come. But runners can't live in the past. Once we quit looking ahead, we become ex-runners. So let me count the ways that I still look—and move—forward:

- Waking up to the first two hours of each day, which usually are my best two in every 24.

- Starting the day by writing a new diary page (where this piece began).

- Greeting the first light of day with a run—or on rest days, with a walk.

- Running in outlandish weather—be it windy, rainy, snowy, cold, or hot.

- Running in the sunshine in the normally wet Oregon winter.

- Running in a downpour in the normally dry Oregon summer.

- Running with my dog, Mingo—the best training partner I've ever had.

- Running long on the trail that honors Steve Prefontaine in the best possible way.

- Running fast on the track at Hayward Field, the "Carnegie Hall" of our sport.

- Going out for one hour, my favorite length of run.

- Taking one-minute walking breaks on long runs.

- Picking up speed while timing a single mile, my favorite distance to go fast.

- Buying freshly baked bagels on the way home from a morning run.

- Eating breakfast, my favorite meal, while reading the morning paper after a run.

- Shaving and showering after the postrun breakfast, while listening to NPR's *Morning Edition.*

- Taking a day off after earning it with a good run.

- Returning to running, hungry for it again, after a good day off.

- Getting over an injury and getting back to normal running.

- Going on the road to talk with runners at a race.

- Coming home from a road trip with a fresh set of memories.

- Racing a 5K, my shortest distance now.

- Racing a half-marathon, my longest that qualifies as a race and not a survival test.

- Planning and training for the next marathon.

- Surviving the latest marathon with no serious aftereffects.

- Visiting the Drake Relays, my ancestral home in this sport.

- Watching high school and college cross-country meets.

- Watching any track meet at Hayward Field.

- Reading anything by my favorite running writers, Kenny Moore and Don Kardong.

- Reading *Track & Field News,* the purists' publication.

- Reading the online *Runner's World* and *Race Results Weekly,* my quickest sources of news.

- Receiving letters, calls, e-mails, or faxes from runners and readers.

The list of joys-to-come could run much longer. But it's long enough already to show that I don't spend all my time looking backward. The past is a nice place to visit, but we can't live there.

Index

Note: Page numbers in *italics* denote photographs.

About the Author

Joe Henderson has made a career of promoting consistency and longevity in running—through his books, his writings in *Runner's World,* and his talks at races. He has lived that message as both a runner and writer.

Born in Illinois in 1943, he began running in Iowa 14 years later. And three years after that, he started writing about the sport. Henderson, a graduate of Drake University, has run more than 700 races. Their distances range from less than 100 meters to more than 100 kilometers.

In addition to his long-time column in *Runner's World,* he has written more than a dozen books on running (listed on opposite page), and he publishes the newsletter *Running Commentary.* He is a former editor of *Runner's World* and a onetime staff writer for *Track & Field News.* The Road Runners Club of America has twice honored him as Journalist of the Year. He also is a member of the RRCA's Hall of Fame.

Henderson runs and writes from his home base in Eugene, Oregon. His wife, Barbara Shaw, is also a published writer.

Books by Joe Henderson

Long, Slow Distance

Road Racers and Their Training

Thoughts on the Run

Run Gently, Run Long

The Long Run Solution

Jog, Run, Race

Run Farther, Run Faster

The Running Revolution

Running, A to Z

Running Your Best Race

Running for Fitness, for Sport and for Life

Joe Henderson's Running Handbook

Total Fitness

Think Fast

Bill Rodgers and Priscilla Welch on Masters Running and Racing (with Bill Rodgers and Priscilla Welch)

Fitness Running (with Richard Brown)

Did I Win?

Better Runs

Marathon Training

Best Runs

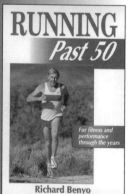

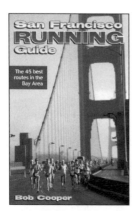
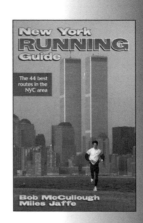